"If this book is like everything else John does, it'll be a best-seller, which irritates me because he's good-looking, funny, *and* clever. It's like he went to the comic buffet and took everything. 'Hey, John, take one item and move on!' He's one of my top three all-time favorite comedians, next to me and Foxworthy. Buy this book—you'll be glad you did. Then check out larrythecableguy.com for all my tour dates."

—LARRY THE CABLE GUY

"What I saw in you was authenticity, and that fascinated me."

—BERT KREISCHER, *Bertcast*

"One of the more important interviews I've conducted was with John Crist. He's absolutely hilarious, one of the funniest people I've ever met!"

—MARTY SMITH, ESPN host and reporter

DELETE THAT

DELETE THAT

(AND OTHER FAILED ATTEMPTS TO LOOK GOOD ONLINE)

JOHN CRIST

CROWN
FORUM

Copyright © 2022 by John Crist

Published in the United States by Crown Forum, an imprint of Random House, a division of Penguin Random House LLC, New York.

CROWN FORUM with colophon is a registered trademark of Penguin Random House LLC.

Hardback ISBN 978-0-593-44521-1
Ebook ISBN 978-0-593-44522-8

Printed in the United States of America on acid-free paper

crownpublishing.com

1st Printing

First Edition

Book design by Debbie Glasserman

To Mom and Dad: For your understanding, care, and love. I'll never forget that one night at home when I came downstairs for dinner and you asked me where I had been sneaking off to all those nights. I finally confessed that I had been going to the comedy club and that one day I wanted to be a stand-up comedian. I can't imagine what that moment must have been like as a parent. I'll never forget the look on Dad's face. From the small bar shows to the arena shows, y'all have been there through all of them. Thank you. I love you both.

To my siblings, Benjamin, Barton, Joseph, Elizabeth, Elias, Emma, and Evangeline: For the conversations that y'all have had to endure that started with, "Wait, your last name is Crist? Are you related to that comedian guy?" And all the subsequent proud, funny, or embarrassing interactions that have come along with sharing the same last name. Thank you. I love you all, and your spouses, and (most of) your kids.

PREFACE

Look at you, out here reading a book! You should feel proud of yourself. Look at all those people around you on their phones or staring at their computer screens or watching TV. But not you—not right now, anyway. You're READING A BOOK! Impressive. Even if you don't learn anything from this book, even if you don't laugh once, at least it's nice to feel superior to anyone who's on their phone right now. I'd call that a win, and we're only one paragraph in.

There is always that one guy at the airport. Everyone is pre-occupied, looking at their phones, but there's always the "book guy." That's you right now. Take a bow.

Airports are big "Look at me, I'm reading a book now!" spots. (Coffee shops are a close runner-up.) And it's always got to be some impressively titled book, just to make the optics look better. I'm over here scrolling through TikTok, and the lady next to me is reading *How to End World Hunger*. And when you board the plane, you've got to carry your book across your chest, cover out, so everyone can see how much of a humanitarian you are. I mean, otherwise, what's the point of reading that book in public?

You want to know one exception to this book-in-airports rule? *The Big Book of Alcoholics Anonymous.* I spent four months in rehab in 2019–2020, and the first thing they give you at check-in is the AA book. Before I even opened the book, I noticed one thing: It's completely coverless. It's just big and blue. Nothing at all on the cover. No title, no subtitle, no author credit, nothing.

I spotted a lady with that big blue book on a flight recently. I whispered to her that I'd read the book too, and we chatted the whole flight, but in low tones, almost as if we were exchanging military secrets. We didn't want anyone to know what we were talking about. I mean, that's why the cover is so nondescript, right? That's why we were whispering. We were supposed to be ashamed. Yet there we were on that flight, talking about what we'd gotten from that book and from our experiences and gathering real strength from it.

I've got an idea: Next time you're reading a book you're embarrassed about, before you leave the house to go to the coffee shop or the airport, just throw a different cover on the book. Sure, you're reading *Fifty Shades of Grey* or *What to Do After a Divorce,* but your cover says *War and Peace* or *The Seven Habits of Highly Effective People.* Boom. It's a win-win. In fact, I think the publishers of those highbrow books could make a killing just selling the covers, without the books. That's my million-dollar idea. And I'm giving it away on page two. Because that's the kind of generous soul I am.

Here's the thing: We're all kinda full of it in that way, aren't we? I'll start with an example. Maybe that will help.

One time I posted an Instagram story from my church on Sunday morning. Later that night, I was drunk at the Red Door Saloon a mile down the street. I did not post about that. In fact, someone tagged a photo of me there, and I untagged myself.

Here's another one.

One time a fan sent me a DM that read, "I struggle with depression, and your comedy has helped me through some hard times." I reposted it and said something like, "This is why I do what I do. #blessedtobeablessing." The same day, I also got a DM from a woman who told me she loved me and sent me a photo of her in her underwear. I didn't repost that one, but I probably looked at it for way longer.

One more?

I'm a stand-up comedian. I've subtly bragged about that on the internet thousands of times. I also have spent significant stretches of time in recent years on antidepressants. I've never posted about that once.

Does that make sense? We're all just out here faking at keeping it real and hoping no one really notices. Was I at church on that Sunday morning? Yes. Was I humbled that my work has helped someone cope with depression? Yes. Am I successful comedian? Yes. All those things are true. But they're not the *whole* truth.

To be loved but not known is comforting but superficial. To be known and not loved is our greatest fear. But to have both? That's perfection.

Timothy Keller said that, and, in essence, that's what this book is about. It's full of funny stories about myself and others, trying to make ourselves look better than we actually are, in appearances, conversations, and on the internet. It's really that simple. Except, of course, it's not that simple at all.

And before we really get going here, one really important thing: Whenever you're reading this book in public, remember to look up every once in a while, for the sole purpose of looking down on the people all around you who are staring slack-jawed at their phones. You're reading a book now. You're better than them. Never forget that.

CONTENTS

INTRODUCTION

GIMME A SEC

Not too long ago, I shared an Instagram story from the McDonald's drive-through. I don't remember what the particular story was about—probably something about how people need to memorize their orders or about the ice cream machine being broken—but it was the responses to that video that really stuck with me:

"First of all, why are you at a McDonald's?"

"Well, that's what you get for eating McDonald's. 🤮"

"Do you have any idea how unhealthy that place is?"

"McDonald's, bro, really? I haven't eaten there since I was ten."

"I'll never eat there again. I legit found a thumb in my McChicken last week!"

Okay, I made that last one up, but here's the point: How come no one will ever own up to eating at McDonald's? How come no one posts a photo of themselves digging into their Big Mac meal deal on Instagram, but they can't stop posting photos of kale salads and cleansing, detoxifying kombucha? According to the internet, the forward-facing version of ourselves, everyone is too good, too healthy, too image conscious to hit the dollar menu at 2:00 A.M.? If we're to believe what most of us see on social media, hardly anyone ever eats at McDonald's. But how is this possible? You can't drive two miles in this country without seeing one. There's literally a McDonald's on every other block. And *every* time I drive past one, the parking lot is full and the drive-through line circles the building.

SOMEONE IS EATING THERE.

Meanwhile, if I were to scroll my Instagram right now, my feed will be littered with pictures of avocado toast, vegan hummus, and some suburbanite preparing a HelloFresh meal. Can we discuss those pre-prepared meal kits, by the way? No one wants to eat quinoa fritters with arugula-strawberry salad and walnuts, much less see your post about how super-awesome it was to make it. We all know that anyone who Ikeas one of those meals together is thinking, I swear if this meal doesn't work out, I'm ordering *a pizza*. But only after they Instagram a photo of themselves assembling it.

It's not just food that we do this with. It's everything. Do you know who the most hated band in America is? Nickelback. They've held that title for decades. It's not even close. They are the punch line to every hack joke about music that everyone hates. But guess what? When Nickelback comes to your town, they're performing at a stadium.

SOMEONE IS LISTENING TO THEM.

Do you see the pattern? I mean, let's look online for five seconds: We claim to be the salad-eating, CrossFitting, charity-giving, small-business-supporting, keto-dieting, indie-band-(before-they-were-famous)-listening, meal-prepping, family-prioritizing, church-attending, Habitat for Humanity–volunteering, no-filter-using, TOMS-wearing, whale-saving, corporate-America-shunning, juice-cleansing, purpose-driven, inclusive, equality-supporting, free-range, fair-trade, environmentally sustainable, gourmet-coffee-sipping group of people.

But in reality, we're also the McDonald's-eating, couch-sitting, tabloid-reading, Walmart-shopping, Top 40–listening, lotto-ticket-buying, beer-drinking, meme-scrolling, *Bachelorette*-bingeing, Kardashian-obsessed, Tinder-swiping, double-chin-having, time-wasting, prejudiced, SUV-driving, mob-tweeting, DM-sliding, bikini-photo-liking, late-night-Postmates-ordering, Pornhub-surfing, *TMZ*-loving, too-lazy-to-recycle group of people.

You know who embodies that dichotomy more than anyone? Me.

This is my story.

This is *Delete That*.

DELETE THAT

1

WANNA HEAR A JOKE?

It was June 12, 2012. I opened my eyes and knew something was wrong. I looked around and could tell I was in a hospital, but I had no idea how I'd gotten there. And I couldn't move. My arms, my legs, and my neck were all strapped to the hospital bed. I legit thought I was about to meet the Lord.

A nurse came to my bedside. She told me I'd been in a car wreck. My silver 1998 Honda Civic had been T-boned by a Dodge Ram—generally not a confrontation that ends well for the Civic. I'd been ejected through the passenger-side window and landed on the road. Hard. When I got to the hospital, I was having seizures, hence the restraints on my wrists, ankles, and neck. The nurse began to ask me questions. "What day is it?" Not sure. "What are your parents' names?" I don't know. "Who is the president?" No idea. Then I passed out again.

When I came to, the scene had changed. Instead of one nurse, now there were at least five doctors and nurses, all gathered around my bed, all looking at me. And they were laughing. I mean, *dying* laughing. I was like, "What is everyone laughing at?" One of the nurses said, "You told us you were a comedian, and you've been telling us all jokes!" Me. Strapped to a hospital bed. Telling jokes. Semiconscious! And, apparently, I was crushing.

Maybe that's when I knew for sure I was on the right path in my life. I don't know if I was born to be a comedian, but certainly, by that point, there was something so deeply ingrained in me that wanted, that needed, to make people laugh that I could do it without even being in control of my faculties. It was almost a primitive, involuntary reflex:

See people.

Make them laugh.

It's not lost on me either that it was a room full of people laughing that snapped me back into consciousness. Laughter, to me, was not just a pleasant diversion. It may have literally saved my life. More on that later.

THANK YOU, TEXT

That was the summer of 2012. At the time, I had recently gotten dumped by the girl I thought I was going to marry, quit a good job in Colorado Springs, and moved to Denver to pursue comedy full time. You ever see that movie *Failure to Launch*? That film was based on that period of my life. Okay, not really, but let's just say that when I saw that movie, I could relate. I was not exactly setting the world on fire.

The afternoon of the accident, I was on my way to a comedy club, the Denver Improv, to let them know my "avails"— essentially, when I'd be available to perform over the coming weeks. I was texting and driving, because, well, of course I was. Around that time, I even had a joke in my set about this: "You ever been texting at a red light and looked up to see that the light was *yellow*?" Meaning you were literally staring at your phone the duration of the green light and didn't look up until it was too late. That was exactly where my head was back then: buried deep in my phone.

And not *just* back then. In truth, if there is anything in my life that operates with nearly the same kind of life-giving power and life-obliterating destructive force as comedy, it's my phone. It is my one trusty companion wherever I go. In those early years of comedy, me and my BlackBerry were inseparable. (Yes, I just said BlackBerry. I don't care what any of y'all say—back in 2010, the BlackBerry was a flex! The president had a Black-Berry. Can't hide money! Well, technically my phone was purchased by the company I worked for, but still.) Anyway, me and that phone were like Tom Sawyer and Huck Finn—minus the racism—traveling the country, exploring new worlds, and learning new things. Except instead of a wooden raft on the Mississippi, I had a Honda Civic with no air-conditioning.

That phone was my best friend. Really. When the affirmation that came with standing on a stage and making people laugh was not readily available to me—because it was, you know, two in the afternoon on a Monday—I could get a fix on my phone, through video views, Instagram likes, Twitter reactions, DMs with fans, or texts with friends. Little electronic shots of love (or what I thought was love). Me and that BlackBerry were in a bur-geoning relationship: It was fun, new, and exciting.

Don't think I don't know how unhealthy this was, and not just because I'm about to get T-boned by a Dodge Ram in this story. My addiction to my phone, my desire to be the person I pretended to be on social media, my need to fill a hole deep in-side me with the attention and approval of others, coupled with a belief that I had to live up to a vision of the perfect Christian that had been drilled into me since birth, would eventually help blow up my entire life in the most public and embarrassing way possible. (More on that later. I promise.) But back at the intersection of Tenth and Logan in downtown Denver in 2012, it was merely about to land me in the emergency room.

To this day, I still have no memory of the impact. They say the force of it knocked out some of my memory. Or maybe it was the force of the trauma. It's all a bit blurry. Either way, a few days after the collision, I called the driver of the other vehicle, a guy named Lance. His phone number was on the police report, so I figured I'd ask him to tell me exactly what happened. When he answered the phone, I said, "Hey, man, it's John, the guy from the car wreck." He was surprised to hear from me. He had called around to several hospitals but couldn't find me. He had assumed the worst, so he was relieved to find out I was alive. I asked him if we could meet back at the site of the accident, which was very close to where I was living, so he could explain what happened. He agreed, and when we met up, he reconstructed it all for me.

He had just started rolling through the intersection, when I blitzed through it, eyes on my phone, running straight through a red light. He hit the side of my car, which then spun out and struck a light post, knocking it to the ground. After I'd been shot out the side window of my Civic, he got out of his pickup truck, walked over, saw me bleeding on the pavement, and assumed I was a goner.

I was pretty bummed to find out from Lance that the paramedics quickly cut all my clothes off me—apparently, that's standard if you're having a seizure—so then not only was I bleeding in the street, but I was doing it naked in front of my neighbors. Yikes. Every night, I lay down to sleep and thank God for my family, for my health, and that those Ring doorbell cameras didn't exist in 2012. Some people like to sleep with clothes on because of the fear that an emergency will force them to run out of the house naked in full view of their neighbors. Well, that essentially happened to me on June 12, 2012. Just add blood. They loaded me into the ambulance, and because I was having a seizure, the medical team worked on me right there, with the ambulance doors open, still at the crash site.

I'd always thought myself to be a much better Christian than I actually was. That's why I was so caught off guard by what happened next.

As Lance recalled the scene to me at that intersection, just days after it had happened, I was still in a bit of a haze. Some of it may have been the painkillers they'd sent home with me from the hospital, but truthfully I felt touched by a certain grace, confident that God was really working in my life. I was going on and on about this to Lance. I told him that I believed God had a plan for me—that his grace sustained my body and that we're all on this planet to glorify him. You know, all the Christian phrases I could slide in. Looking back, I probably should have told him I ran the light because I was reading the Bible on my phone, not texting. Anyway, I was going on about how I was a Christian and that I felt it was a genuine miracle I was still alive. He took it all in and nodded thoughtfully.

"You're a Christian, huh?" he asked.

"Yes," I confirmed.

"That's interesting," he said, "because when you were in the ambulance, I was standing right outside the back of it, giving my statement to the police. You were apparently in a lot of pain, and you were screaming the loudest, longest barrage of f-bombs I've ever heard in my whole life."

Oops.

So, the two things I learned about myself from this car wreck: When my subconscious is on autopilot, I'm going to tell jokes, and I'm apparently going to cuss—loudly. Both of those things are deep in me on a primal level that I don't totally understand, and as many other things in my life have taught me, we can't hide from who we really are. But we sure do try.

I've spent most of my adult life attempting to hide from who I really am, trying to bury the less flattering parts of myself under a mountain of sarcastic jokes, carefully staged Instagram posts, and well-deployed hair product. It took a figurative car crash in my personal life—which in its own way left me, essentially, bleeding and naked by the side of the road—for me to begin to understand and accept the real me. Who, as it turns out, is just a pretty normal guy who cusses sometimes and probably looks at his phone way too much. In fact, if you're like me, a lot of the cussing is because of what we see on our phones.

By the way, after I got out of the hospital in Denver, I went to the wreck yard to inspect my car after the accident. You know, that traumatizing experience that reminds you of your poor choices. My car was totaled, destroyed completely beyond repair. Windows all blown out, engine exposed, hubcaps missing, and the frame utterly mangled. I managed to peel open the driver's door, and sitting there on the floor, in front of the passenger seat, was my phone, still charged, without a scratch on it, blowing up with notifications. Which, of course, made me feel much better.

2

UNTAG ME

If you search my profile on Twitter, it's pristine. If you search my name on Twitter, it's more of a mixed bag. The timeline is pretty. The mentions tell a different story.

On Instagram, it's pretty much the same. Shoot, my feed is almost superhuman. I bet if you click on it now, there's a photo of me doing stand-up at a big theater. Maybe there's a tour poster with red "Sold out!" banners over most of the dates, likely a funny video that I recently posted, and maybe an advertisement for a comedy festival or celebrity golf tournament that I'm taking part in or something. You get the idea: My Instagram is a humblebrag of sorts. Maybe not even that humble of a brag. Just my attempt to get the world to think that I'm successful, however subtly or unsubtly I attempt to do it.

If you toggle from my posts to the ones I'm tagged in by other people, well, there you start to get a slightly more realistic portrait of who I really am. There's me performing at my friend's open-mic night to an audience of about a dozen people. There's me at an airport posing for a photo with a fan, with bags under my eyes, looking a full mess, but the caption reads "I just met the funniest guy on earth @johnbcrist!" And there I am at 1:30 A.M. in downtown Nashville making a goofy face with my arms around a group of fans I just met. There are probably a few photos of old jokes I told in there, still tagged, as long as they've aged well, obviously. So now we're getting a little warmer.

But there is a third category of Instagram posts. These are the posts that really get to the core of who somebody really is. Fortunately or unfortunately, these are the posts you can't see, because they're the ones that have been *un*tagged.

It's a funny idea, the idea of untagging yourself in a photo. Basically, you look at the photo and then decide whether or not you want people knowing *that* side of you. It clearly *is* you, so it's a truthful, sincere version of you, but you get to decide if you want other people seeing that truthful, sincere version of you.

One time, someone recognized me in a Walgreens while I was getting some anti-itch cream. No lie. We took a photo in the aisle with all the skin-rash treatments, and I was glued to my Instagram for the next twenty minutes waiting for her to post the pic so I could untag myself. I didn't want people to see me looking like hot garbage, nor did I particularly want the world to know about my athlete's foot. Was I in the personal-care aisle? Yes. Would I have preferred the photo to be taken in the candy aisle? Also, yes.

DELETE YOUR HISTORY

I know I'm not the only one who has done this kind of thing. So many of us are selectively curating our social media accounts to present a very particular version of ourselves to the world. That's kind of the whole point of social media. Instagram and

Facebook are filled with meal-prep photos and videos—people creating these amazing, sustainably sourced, organic, gluten-free feasts for their family. How come nobody is tagging themselves sitting alone with a fried-shrimp platter at Captain D's?

It's like that Timothy Keller line I mentioned earlier: "To be loved but not known is comforting but superficial. To be known and not loved is our greatest fear. But to have both? That's perfection." He kind of nailed it. I wonder what it would be like if people knew me as the fun, energetic comedian *and* the guy who struggles with depression and loneliness. That's scary to even type! The guy who goes to the gym *and* also Uber-Eats McDonald's at midnight. The guy who sells out comedy shows *and* also gets secretly jealous of other comedians' success. That quote sounds nice—it really does—but often it seems practically impossible to achieve.

I doubt I'm alone in feeling this. Untagging has become a lifestyle: Wake up, brush teeth, and untag yourself from all the photos from the previous night that you don't want your mother, your boss, your friends, or even complete strangers to see. This is how I lived for a long time. Raise your hand if you have too. (Unless you're listening to this as an audiobook and holding a baby and making pottery or operating heavy machinery. In that case, please don't feel the need to raise your hand.)

Don't worry: This is not the point where I launch into my book-length rant about the dangers of social media. I love social media. I'd be unemployed without social media. As I write this sentence, I'm sitting in a house purchased with money I made thanks to social media. In the words of Garth Brooks, "You'll never hear me complain!" Except that of course you will.

Everyone complains about social media. In fact, there's almost nothing more common on social media than people complaining about social media. If I hear one more influencer complain about the evils of Instagram, while simultaneously maintaining an Instagram account with a million followers, I'm going to lose my mind.

No one needed to watch a Netflix documentary to know that social media is toxic and is warping our brains. If you spend ten minutes scrolling through TikTok, you'll come to the exact same conclusion. But if you go back in history, anytime there has been a world-changing technology—telephones, cars, the printing press—I guarantee there were also many people getting irrationally upset about it. I'm old enough to remember when everyone used to tell us that TV is rotting our brains. Now it's referred to as "prestige television." Watching *Better Call Saul* or *The Crown* is seen as the cultural equivalent to reading Shakespearean sonnets. I hear people bragging about how many times they've watched *The Sopranos,* as if it's an intellectual exercise to sit on the couch and watch people murder each other on TV. All I'm saying is, give it time and I'm sure we'll one day be putting Twitter threads and TikTok videos into the Smithsonian.

At this point, decrying social media and the internet is kind of like shouting at the wind. It's there, it's not going anywhere, and it's certainly not going anywhere because you're shouting at it. So we adapt or perish, right? And watching all of us try to sort that out—trying to figure out how to be the people we claim to be on the internet, how to hide the bits of ourselves we don't want anyone to see—*that* is funny. So that's where I come in. I'm not shouting at the wind; I'm laughing at it and trying to make you do the same.

▉ UNTAGGING: A SHORT HISTORY

I was in the grocery store recently, and someone glanced in my cart and asked me, "Oh, how old are your kids?" I looked down in my cart, and it was filled with all my favorite foods: Doritos, gummy worms, frozen pizzas, and string cheese. Of course, I don't have any kids, but I realized it was time to get more strategic about my grocery shopping. Produce stays on the top. Either junk food gets shoved to the bottom or I just buy it at the end so I'm not a grown man rolling around Kroger with Lunchables in my cart. I asked my Instagram followers if they could relate, and tons of people chimed in to say they do the same thing. "I work at a church and I always hide the wine in my cart!" "I'm a schoolteacher. I don't want my students to see me buy condoms." Okay, so I'm not the only one? I feel better already!

Look, it's not like the urge to untag ourselves is new. It was not invented in the social media era. Anonymous sources essentially have been untagging themselves in newspaper stories for decades. More than 70 percent of Congress voted to authorize the war in Iraq in 2002, but once that became a quagmire (not the *Family Guy* character), most of them couldn't untag themselves from that authorization resolution fast enough.

Shoot, read the story of Peter in the Bible. He was essentially doing the same thing. After Jesus was arrested, his disciple and friend Peter denied knowing him—three times. First, a servant girl saw Peter sitting around a campfire and recognized him as one of Jesus's crew. "This man was with him," the girl said. "Woman, I don't know him," Peter insisted. Then this servant girl again said she was sure she saw him hanging around with Jesus. Again, Peter pretended he didn't know what she was talking about. Another servant finally got specific and asked Peter, "Didn't I see you with him in the olive garden?" Still, Peter was like, "No way! Not me. Jesus? Never heard of the guy." To be fair to Peter, nobody really wants to be tagged in the Olive Garden, although the breadsticks there are pretty fire.

The big push to take down statues and monuments all over the country these days is kind of a mass untagging of this country from its sometimes-problematic history. Essentially, anytime there's a push to rename a building or holiday, we are trying to untag ourselves. It's as if the whole country woke up bleary eyed one morning, a little hungover, and scrolled back through its feed, slightly horrified: Christopher Columbus was a genocidal madman (untag!); Thomas Jefferson impregnated one of his slaves (untag!); we booted Native Americans off their land (untag!). But untagging ourselves doesn't change history, whether we're talking about the Bay of Pigs invasion or the four double vodka shots we had last night. It happened.

Don't get me wrong: This sort of untagging is not *always* a bad impulse. I spent some time in rehab in 2020—if this is the first you're hearing of this, just wait—at a facility in Hattiesburg, Mississippi, associated with Forrest General Hospital. The place is named after Nathan Bedford Forrest. Who, you may ask, is this Nathan Bedford Forrest? The esteemed Mr. Forrest was a Confederate general, the first grand wizard of the Ku Klux Klan, and—from what I can tell by reading his Wikipedia page—not a great guy by today's standards, and one who would certainly qualify for social media cancellation. But also, that hospital saved my life, so I don't know. It makes my existence feel like a never-ending comedy bit. My life was saved at a hospital in Mississippi named after the first grand wizard of the KKK. I will refrain from writing the jokes that puts in my head.

Should the name of that hospital be changed? That seems like a reasonable idea. But it seems like there's something new to cancel every day. I wonder if our collective hypervigilance is going too far. In San Francisco, the school board was considering renaming Abraham Lincoln High School because of Lincoln's attitude toward Native Americans and because through his policies and rhetoric, our sixteenth president apparently "did not show . . . that Black lives ever mattered" to him. I am not making this up. That is the actual quote. This is the same guy who signed the Emancipation Proclamation, led the Union through a war that ended slavery, and, oh by the way, got assassinated for his trouble. Maybe we should cut the dude some slack.

I hear some of you shouting at the pages of this book, *John, but what does any of this have to do with me? I didn't name that hospital or that school. I didn't vote to authorize the Iraq War.* All I'm saying is that the urge to hide the things we're not proud of is totally human. I should know. I spent years polishing my public image, untagging myself from the more unflattering parts of my life, pretending I was some sort of wisecracking, squeaky-clean Christian superhero role model, when, in fact, I was actually just a regular ol' deeply flawed human.

I don't think I'm the only one who has been floundering as I try to square the person I claim to be with the person I actually am. I mean, have you ever posted photos of you and your friends partying on the weekend but made the setting "close friends only" because you didn't want your boss to see them?

Have you ever untagged yourself from a photo in which you were wearing a low-cut top and doing tequila shots, because you didn't want the disapproving comments from your mother-in-law? I'm not saying that doing tequila shots is some sort of crime against humanity—most would argue the opposite, actually—but you get my point.

Sidenote: One time early in my career in Salt Lake City of all places, a heavily intoxicated woman came to the postshow meet-and-greet wielding a Sharpie and asked me if I would sign her boobs. I thought, *I'm not Axl Rose; I'm a homeschooled pastor's kid who sometimes performs in churches.* Did I want to do it? You bet. Did I want to be photographed doing it? Absolutely not.

Tagging and untagging existed long before social media gave us a name for it. Think about a politician visiting sick kids in hospitals or cutting a ribbon at the opening of a new stadium or donning a hard hat and pretending to bro down with some construction workers he'd otherwise never bother speaking to. Those photo ops are just a politician saying, "Tag me here, doing this thing that makes me look like someone you'd want to vote for." I'm not mad at them—at least not for that.

If you think this is an activity reserved for politicians or people who get followed around by news crews, remember the last time you ran into a famous person in public. What's the first thing you did? That's right—you ran up with your phone and took a picture of yourself alongside this celebrity. But think about it: Why? What is the impulse that pushes us to do this? (And I'm as guilty as anyone. I do it too!) Who do we think we're fooling? I mean, do you ever look at the photo your friend posted of herself with Luke Bryan at the airport on Instagram and think, *Wow. I didn't realize Lindsey was so tight with Luke Bryan. I wonder where they're going together?*

It's a weird concept when you break it down, but it's existed for a long time. You go into a diner, and on the wall by the register, there is almost always a collection of photos of famous people eating there. *Why,* though? Are we meant to believe that Vin Diesel is an expert on where to get the best patty melts in Cincinnati and he chose that very place? Or perhaps that if Newt Gingrich, 2 Chainz, and Ryan Reynolds all ate there, it must have something for everyone? Or maybe just that the place is strictly for ballers?

I suppose people just want to feel special or at the very least want other people to think they're special. Think about what we've done to the process of getting on an airplane. Remember when we used to board by rows? No one felt special then. But now we've got separate boarding calls for Medallion, Platinum Medallion, Diamond Medallion, First Class, Business Class, Sky Priority, Comfort Plus, and Zone 1. It's crazy to me that people are at the gate fighting to get on the plane as early as possible. And why are they doing this? To spend more time in a too-small seat, breathing stale air, next to armrest-hogging strangers? At this point, they ought to start boarding people at the gate by name over the loudspeakers like they are being introduced as one of the starting five at an NBA game. "And sitting in seat 24B, a five-foot-seven staff accountant from Minneapolis, Joooooel Peterson!" Actually, now that I think about it, if they called my name like that, I'd be way into it.

Appearances are everything, especially these days. Entire industries have grown up around both maintaining them and tearing them down, particularly online. That's the whole business of search engine optimization (SEO). You hire a company to game the results of a Google search so search results that enhance your or your business's reputation are pushed to the top and the ones that are less favorable are buried. (*Sets reminder to call one.*) This is an industry that is basically built on being very selective and strategic in its tagging. So, those records of your restaurant's failed health examinations? Consider them gone. That story about how all the C-suite execs at some company were caught fudging the accounting reports and dodging taxes? It's like it never happened! Any crappy motel can suddenly look like the Ritz-Carlton in its search results. Any janky fruit stall can pass itself off as being better than Whole Foods.

Increasingly, people are giving themselves the SEO treatment. In Europe, there is actually something called "the right to be forgotten," where you can go through a legal process to have information you don't like removed from the internet. Recently, a handful of newspapers in the United States have started allowing people to submit forms to ask the paper to disappear unflattering news stories about themselves. It's like you can actually erase history. It's the ultimate in untagging!

PIC OR IT DIDN'T HAPPEN

A few years back, I was doing a comedy show at a church in Texas. For those of you who didn't realize you could do comedy in a church, who thought that stand-up was literally the antithesis of church, it's not. In fact, it's not that different from doing stand-up in a club—just take out the swear words and add some soccer moms. Anyway, on this particular night, I was doing this show, and if you know anything about churches in

Texas, they're like most everything in Texas: big. That night, the connection with the crowd was particularly close, and when that happens, I start to feel really comfortable and can get off track. I really riff. For whatever reason, I went off on a little bit of a slightly earnest tangent about porn and how it was a problem for me for a long time in my life. I don't know why I started talking about it, but I think the riff was funny and honest. Maybe too honest. At the conclusion of my little rant, I tried to throw a lifeline to other people who were struggling with porn habits: "If any of you here have any questions or want to talk in person, come to the merch table after the show and I'm happy to talk to you about it."

After most shows back in those days, the merch table was swamped with hundreds of people buying stuff, talking to me, snapping photos. After this show, literally no one came to the table. Not a soul. People were going out of their way to walk around the auditorium to avoid even being seen in the vicinity of the merch table. I remember my manager calling me afterward and saying, "I'm looking at the numbers from the Texas show and we didn't sell any merch last night. What happened?"

I sighed. "Well," I said, "I might have told everyone that if they were addicted to porn to see me at the merch table. I guess that was a bad idea."

I learned an important lesson that day: There are certain places nobody wants to be seen, and in line to talk to someone about their porn addiction is definitely one of them. I suppose that's understandable. For most people, watching a lot of porn is shameful. Here's a fact though: Porn is one of the biggest industries in the whole entire world. It is a $97 billion business. Porn makes up about 30 percent of all business on the internet.

Porn sites get more traffic each month than Amazon, Netflix, and Twitter combined. I mean, it's just like with the McDonald's and Nickelback examples I gave earlier: Clearly, *somebody* is watching it!

This phenomenon cuts both ways. If there are certain places no one wants to be tagged—in line for help with their porn addiction, at a fast-food drive-through after midnight, getting their mugshot taken after a DUI—there are also places where everyone wants to be, and it often makes no more logical sense. A couple of years ago, I performed on the Winter Jam Spectacular, which is a massive Christian-music arena tour (plus me, apparently, that year). Everyone always wanted to go backstage on that tour. Even my friends and family. People absolutely loved to go to the side of the stage, flash their VIP all-access guest pass around their neck to two meaty-looking security dudes in yellow jackets, and then be allowed into the bowels of whatever arena we were in. Guess what there was backstage? Nothing. Just some crew guys packing up road cases, and the catering people breaking down what was left of dinner. Didn't matter. People loved it.

Look, I know the feeling. It feels good to be preferred, to be seen, to sit in first class, to skip the line, and to have the courtside seats. Is the experience better? Marginally. Are the optics better? You bet! Does it make you *feel* special? Absolutely.

Ironically enough, while all the fans were clamoring to get themselves backstage, some of the performers, including me, would often drive twenty-five minutes across town after the shows for fear of being spotted by fans doing something— having a couple of beers—that we did not want to be caught doing. Mind you, we weren't underage or even getting very wild, but there we would be, stealthily climbing into an Uber and then shoving ourselves into the booth at the back of an Applebee's so we could drink a few Coors Lights. There was nothing particularly shameful about our actions—well, okay, maybe the hanging-out-at-Applebee's part is kind of lame—but we were going to all this trouble because *other* people might not approve. In retrospect, the only thing I feel bad about is that I cared so much what everyone else thought. Because really, when you dig beneath all the untagging, all the deleted history, all the image management, online or in real life, *that* is the impulse that drives it.

3

LIKE AND SUBSCRIBE

When I was growing up, every fall my parents would (literally) shoehorn me and my siblings into clean clothes and force us to smile for a photographer in order to take our annual Christmas card photo. There was always a theme. We might all be in denim, or khaki. I'm sorry to report that there were often props too. With ten of us, these photo shoots were unbearable: "*Please,* tuck in your shirt!" "Really? You forgot to wear a belt?" "You didn't even brush your hair!" "Just stand still for thirty seconds." "Move your leg in." "Tilt your head this way." "No, your boyfriend cannot be in the photo." "Squeeze in and act like you love each other!" A couple of years ago, I actually made a video called "Every Family Christmas Photo Shoot" that went viral. See, traumatic life experiences can be used for good! Who knew?

The resulting photo, along with a family "year in review" that was spin-doctored so heavily it would make a paid political strategist queasy, was then mailed out to friends, family, relatives, church congregants, and so on. This was social media before there was social media. You got one "post" per year, so you had to make it count. Getting your holiday card posted on someone else's fridge was the pre-internet equivalent of a like. But social media is similar to the postal carrier backing up a truck of Christmas cards, dumping them in your front yard, then ringing your doorbell until you come out and look at all of them. *Every day.* This pixilated parade of your friends' perfect lives is practically inescapable. The fact that their perfection is a lie—and you know it's a lie—somehow doesn't keep the jealousy and self-flagellation at bay.

It's funny, I write about the Crist family Christmas card tradition in the past tense, but it endures to this day, and it hasn't changed much. The card's annual family report still represents a weird alternate reality. Each child still gets a little section that recaps their past year: career achievements, marriages, new babies, college graduations. But when someone gets divorced, when someone has health problems, when someone (me) goes to rehab, that is conspicuously left out. I'm sure most families do the same thing. Frankly, I'd enjoy reading someone's honest Christmas card: "Hayden is four. She never eats her vegetables and is brutally defiant, borderline demon-possessed. Jaxon is our precocious ten-year-old. He still wets his bed, which is alarming, but we can't afford a child therapist. Melissa is unhappily married to Jim, who is still working on his anger-management issues. We drink a lot to cope." Okay, admittedly, that would be sad to read, but I'd respect it and for sure hang it on my refrigerator!

ANTISOCIAL MEDIA

Of course, social media has now evolved long past a yearly Christmas card. It all started so simply with Facebook. (Okay, maybe it technically started with things like Myspace and Friendster, but those were before my time.) Facebook made it easy to update your friends, your family, your acquaintances, and people who you were one day hoping to hook up with about how great your life was going. You could post photos and videos—of your beautiful car, of your new haircut, of your kid graduating from high school, of the charity that you were volunteering for—and then include a long heartfelt explanation of what it all meant to you. Innocuous enough, I suppose.

Then Twitter came along and refined that formula with a simple idea: No one cares about your long heartfelt explanations. Sum it up for us in 140 (later 280) characters, because we've got other things to do. Instagram offers an even more brutal take: Stop talking. Just show us the photos. Snapchat, even worse: Show us the photo, and as soon as we're done viewing it, it will disappear forever.

Throughout this evolution, social media's core principle remained largely unchanged: Here is an efficient way to show the whole world exactly the person you *pretend* to be. Even now, most posts are just some version of that, or an ad for the thing you googled a few hours ago.

When I lived in L.A., I went on a date once with someone I met on Snapchat. We had exchanged photos, but she had used so many filters on the photos she'd sent me that when we met up in person, I did not recognize her. At all. I was pretty annoyed and felt like I had been misled, but then I started thinking about how awful she must have felt. I mean, she was so uncomfortable in her own skin that she had to filter herself and manage her appearance in the hope of attracting my attention, to the point where when the real her came out, she was unrecognizable. In some ways, she was just pushing what all of us seem to be doing to its logical extreme.

A couple of years ago, the rapper/actor Bow Wow posted photos to his Instagram of the private jet he was about to take to New York. The only problem was, some clever social media sleuth spotted him that same day flying coach to New York on a commercial flight. The internet lit him up for that, but, again, it was just a case of somebody pushing the acceptable level of social media deception a little further. In fact, there are tons of companies now that will rent you a grounded private jet for an hour so you can come aboard, snap some photos of yourself living the good life, and then post them to Instagram to impress a bunch of people who don't know you well enough to know that you fly Southwest.

Not long ago, stories like those would've sounded crazy, across the line. Today, they seem totally unsurprising. It seems like every day I read about some Instagram model taking snapshots of herself living it up in the lush first-class cabin of a 747 before returning to her actual seat, thirty rows back, near the bathrooms. There's no earthly reason to be mad at someone like that anymore. That's become the norm. You know what sounds crazy now? I heard Bill Hader being interviewed recently, and he mentioned that he's not on social media at all. No Instagram, no Twitter, no Facebook, no TikTok, no nothing. I mean, what's wrong with him? How does he live his life? Does he actually go places just to, you know, *have fun*? Does he just go around being satisfied with life without letting anyone know how satisfied with life he is? Is that even allowed anymore? I mean, what's the point?

I know women who, when they break up with a guy, will

carry out what I like to call the Purge. They literally erase their ex-boyfriend from all their social media accounts. I don't mean just unfollowing him on Instagram, Twitter, TikTok, etc. They've got to unfollow *his* friends and friends they met through *his* friends. Then they go back in their timelines, and any photo with him in it, any reference to him, any *anything* related to him is purged from virtual existence. It's as if he never happened. If you've been dating someone for a year or two, this is not some ten-minute exercise. It's a serious undertaking that could take the better part of a day or two. It doesn't matter if you broke up with him: Are you Insta broken up? That's the real signifier.

FELT CUTE, MIGHT DELETE LATER

In 2014, there was a report that estimated that people uploaded an average of 1.8 billion photos to social media every day. And that was 2014. I'm sure it's many more now. I don't know how many of those 1.8 billion photos actually get viewed by anyone—including the person who took them—but there is no doubt we are looking at more photos than we ever have at any time in history. How many images do you think you look at in a day on Facebook or Instagram? Maybe I'm on social media more than most people, but if you told me I looked at a thousand photos a day, that would seem about right. At any rate, that's a lot of input. I read somewhere that the internet allows you to feel every possible human emotion inside of twenty seconds. You can be happy, depressed, angry, thrilled, turned on, disgusted, jealous, and inspired all in less time than it takes to microwave a Hot Pocket. I don't think our minds are suited for that kind of perpetual emotional roller coaster.

Now throw your own neediness and neuroses into the mix. Start posting the photos from your life, the stories from your day, and the jokes you think are funny. Man, it feels good when those likes start stacking up, doesn't it? I should speak for myself: It absolutely feels really good. I'm sure you can relate. It provides a real dopamine rush to the pleasure center in your brain. The thing is, dopamine doesn't know right from wrong. Dopamine doesn't care whether you are posting your mom's pot roast recipe or election disinformation. It just wants engagement, reaction, buzz, attention. It just needs a hit. Why is this starting to sound more and more like one of those documentaries about drug addiction?

We all do some shameful things chasing that rush. Hey, I'm the king of it. We've all seen those photos of dudes in front of cars they claim to own, weight they claim to have just lifted, or that large horned animal they claim to have just killed. Okay, I haven't done any of *that,* but you get it. Women do it too. Sometimes in the middle of winter, one of them will post a photo from the previous summer, wearing a bikini, looking good, with the caption "Miss the lake days!" or maybe "Can't wait to go back!" What's happening in reality? You're home alone on a Thursday night watching reality TV, eating a frozen dinner in sweatpants, and feeling bad about yourself. A little dopamine bump before bed would be nice. So you scroll back to find a good photo, and likes flood in. The DMs from guys you haven't talked to in a while start buzzing. It's a short-term fix. Trust me, I knooooow. I've done it a million times. Well, maybe not a photo of me in a bikini—though, no doubt, that would draw *some* kind of attention—but I'd be lying if I said I haven't posted things just for that great feeling. You know what would be wild? If someone posted a thirst trap like that and the caption said "I'm gonna be honest. I'm feeling a little lonely and depressed right now. And, honestly, two hundred likes on this photo would make me feel better." That's the kind of transparency I can get behind.

How about this one: Have you ever seen a photo of a girl looking absolutely amazing, not a hair out of place, big smile, makeup done perfectly, gazing off into the distance with the caption "When you remember that you only have pizza rolls at home!" or something ridiculous like that? Oh, please. You know you look good. I'd *die* if someone did that and the caption was "You know I look good right now. Is this outfit, lighting, and filter enough to convince you to like this photo?"

I recognize this behavior only because I'm completely guilty of it myself. I'll give you a perfect example. A while back, I was on *Fox & Friends* in New York City—a *big* TV show. I'm not just going to post a pic and say "Proud to be on *Fox & Friends*" because that makes it look like I'm bragging. So I posted the pic and included a caption about how embarrassed I was that I wore the same shirt on the show that they used in the promo video to intro me. Same idea. Flexing, but trying to act like I'm not. I think I'm being sly about it, but let's be honest: Everyone surely sees through it, because we all do the same thing!

ARE YOU NOT ENTERTAINED?

It's really bizarre when you think about it: Our self-worth is completely wrapped up in the approval of others, most of whom are virtual, if not actual, strangers to us. And this is going on *all the time*. It's like we've all become gladiators in a Roman colosseum waiting for the digital emperor to pass judgment on us. And at the same time, we are that emperor passing judgment on others. Thumbs-up or thumbs-down? Like? Love? Smiley-face emoji? Comment? Ignore? Our fate is in the hands of the same internet mob we are a part of.

I saw a post recently that blew my mind. I mean, it did but it also didn't. A couple who had built up an impressive Instagram following by sharing snapshots and stories from their travel adventures fell off a cliff at Yosemite National Park while inching toward the edge . . . to take . . . a selfie. They fell eight hundred feet and *died*. DIED! For a selfie. For an Instagram post. For more likes. No one forced them to do this. The gladiators in ancient Rome had no choice. But here we are, out there voluntarily putting ourselves in the ring in front of the emperor, choosing to subject ourselves to this public scrutiny. And for what? The internet doesn't care about us. So, why are we loyal to it? (If I could use emojis in this book, I'd insert the syringe one right here.) It's all for the hit.

Before you hurt your neck from shaking your head in judgment at people who would die trying to capture the perfect selfie, I want to ask you a question: Have you ever gotten one of those email notifications from Facebook or another social media platform informing you that you'd been tagged in a photo? Of course you have. And what did you do as soon as you got that notification? That's right, you opened Facebook to see that photo you'd been tagged in. Do you look okay? Were you having a bad-hair day? Do you look fat? Are you hanging out with someone you shouldn't be? Are you doing something you don't want your mom, spouse, pastor, or friends to see? Do you need to untag yourself?

The people who run Facebook aren't dumb. They want you

on their platform *all the time*. When you're not, they are going to lure you back in by playing on your insecurities and your fear of being seen in some way you didn't want to be seen. Everyone's biggest fear is that something they were doing in private is now going to be public.

Sometimes you don't even need to see that notification. Social media has already implanted in us the ultimate FOMO (fear of missing out). We walk around worried that we may not see something being said about us on social media or might miss something important that's happening on the internet. I can think of countless times that I've been out with friends or family, let's say on a hike or on a boat—somewhere where pulling out your phone seems wrong. If an hour or so goes by, I always find myself thinking, *I wonder what's happening on the internet right now*. Scary. You know the only place I don't feel that frantic check-the-phone pull? Onstage, when I'm performing. Although that's probably because I'm getting an even more intense dopamine rush when I'm up there.

Look, I'm not trying to convince anyone to quit social media. (If you're going to, please at least post a couple of pictures of yourself reading this book first.) But if after thinking about it, you're still sure that you need to quit Facebook or Twitter or Instagram or TikTok or whatever other social media obsession might be gripping you, fine, just go ahead and do it. I've done it myself a bunch of times. Sometimes for a week. Sometimes for a month. One time for eight months! And somehow, miraculously, I survived! But please, whatever you do, I beg you, do not post to social media to tell the world that you're quitting social media. I crack up laughing at these people who announce their social media fasts like they're David Letterman doing his final episode of the *Late Show*. I'm like, *We all know it's a drug. You ain't going anywhere. We'll see you on Netflix next year, Dave.*

The power of addiction is overwhelming. The need for affirmation is primal. It's not that easy to just give up. But look at you now: You've just completed another chapter of AN ACTUAL BOOK. You should be proud of yourself. Now you can take a break and check your phone before you start the next one. I know you're dying to.

4

ACROSS THE LINE

I like church. Always have, always will. It almost doesn't matter what the specific church is. Of course, there are outliers—pastors with private jets, snake-handling churches, Westboro Baptist Church—but for the most part, I like any church where you can find people who will welcome you into their community and treat you like one of their own. Which, in my experience, is most churches.

My dad was a pastor, and I loved hanging out at church. Sunday morning, Sunday night, Wednesday-night youth group—it seemed like we were always there, and I couldn't have been happier about it.

In fact, that's how my comedy career started. In church. I did this skit about going on mission trips (really, more of an advertisement to get people to go on our church's summer mission trips) and people laughed so hard that they asked me to do another one, and another one, and another one. But once I started performing in actual comedy clubs, I consciously stripped my jokes of all Christian references. It wasn't that I was ashamed of being a Christian; I just kind of wanted to fit in with the other

comedians. And I'd never really heard an overtly Christian comedian in any of those clubs. I'd certainly heard a million comedians talk about Jesus and church and faith, but never in any sort
of positive way. In fact, when I was living in Los Angeles, my
agent or someone like that told me to trim all the stuff about
church and the Bible from my act. So I did. I just pulled all that
out and joked about normal stuff: texting and driving, the challenges of dating, and living with roommates. (By the way, am I
the only one who can't believe that the idea of college roommates still exists? You just show up one day and they're like,
"This is the guy you'll be living with in a ten-by-ten-foot box
for the next *year* of your life. Good luck!" It blows my mind
that that policy still exists.)

Early in my career, when I had about five pretty decent minutes of this sort of material, I was backstage at the Comedy &
Magic Club, near Los Angeles, and a comic—I wish I could
remember who she was—was onstage doing a bit about Moses
and the burning bush. And it was murdering. I stood backstage
watching and was so confused. Everyone knew exactly what
she was talking about, and they were all laughing. And mind
you, this wasn't in Middle America—this was in L.A., not exactly a hotbed of evangelical Christianity. When she came offstage, I looked at her, dumbfounded.

"What was that?" I asked her.

She looked at me like I was an idiot. "You mean the story of
Moses and the burning bush? It's in the Old Testament."

"No, no, no, I know all that," I said. "I know the story. I just
thought audiences wouldn't get it."

"Everyone knows that story, and if they don't, they can pick
up on the context clues and the jokes still work," she said, and

then she walked off casually. That moment changed my whole career.

It seems so obvious now. It's almost embarrassing to admit that it took me seeing her perform that burning-bush bit to make me realize that my comedy life and my Christian life didn't have to live completely separately. I mean, as of this writing, nearly 70 percent of Americans call themselves Christians, so that's about 230 million people in this country alone who likely have at least some knowledge about this stuff. And even if you're not a Christian—raise your hand and please come forward for prayer—you probably know the basics: There was a guy named Jesus. He did miracles. We read a book called the Bible. We go to these meetings on Sundays at these places called churches. Churches ask you for money. Joel Osteen wants you to live your best life, etc., and so on. Anyway, I remember making a conscious decision that night on the way home from the Comedy & Magic Club to start talking about the real me onstage—who I really was.

Around this same time, I heard an interview with one of the greats: Jerry Seinfeld, Chris Rock, or one of those guys. He said something about how if you want to be a transcendent comedian, you have to write about what you know distinctly. Write the jokes that *only you* can tell. Jokes no one could ever steal because they're so bound up in who you are. Jim Gaffigan writes jokes about being fat, having six kids, and being Catholic. I don't have any jokes about any of that stuff because I'm not any of those things. But Gaffigan doesn't have any jokes about kissing a girl behind the dumpster while working a summer job at Chick-fil-A in Lilburn, Georgia. (How's that for living your *best* life?) Anyone can riff on bad airplane food or how the side effects of prescriptions are often worse than the illnesses they're supposed to cure, but great comedians invite you into *their* world, which in turn usually speaks to *your* world in a meaningful way. And I wanted to be great.

So I started talking about church in the comedy clubs. I talked about growing up as a homeschooled Christian kid. I threw in some Bible references. And almost immediately, the laughs got harder. *Way* harder. My set expanded. I started to get better spots, more bookings, way more opportunities.

All this had a weird side effect that I started noticing. I'd often be walking out of a comedy club after a good set, and audience members would come up to me, quietly pull me aside, and say things like, "Hey man, we really appreciate what you're doing in there." At first, I didn't totally get what they meant, but it quickly became clear that they thought I was on some stealth mission to go into the dark places, among the drunks and the sinners, and spread the gospel. I never really knew how to react to these people, other than to just sort of shrug and say, "Uhh, yeah. Thanks for coming." Because the thing is, regardless of whether I was performing at the Comedy Works in Denver or the Grove City Church of the Nazarene in Columbus, Ohio, spreading the gospel was never what I was trying to do. My comedy is not a sermon. I'm not out there trying to save souls. I mean, I'm not *not* trying to save souls, but you get it. It's all about making people laugh.

I also knew that the quickest path to getting better as a stand-up was in clubs, not churches. If you're a comic who has forged his act playing for churchgoers, it will show. At a comedy club, nobody cares if you're a good Christian or a nice guy. If you're not funny, they'll boo you out. Trust me—it has happened to me. Club audiences are notoriously unforgiving, whereas forgiveness is generally one of the founding principles of a church. (And if it's not at yours, you may want to consider a new church.)

When you bomb at a club, you know it immediately: It gets deathly quiet, you hear the waitstaff taking orders and people shuffling in their chairs, and the moment you get offstage, everyone avoids you like the plague. When you bomb at a church, you might never know it: Everyone still cheers and congratulates you.

RULES ARE RULES

There is a very specific language we speak at church, and not everyone knows it. I once asked my friend Vinnie, who is a great stand-up, to open for me in front of a very churchy crowd. I came up in the Denver comedy scene with Vinnie, and he makes me laugh more than just about anyone else I know. But Vinnie didn't grow up in church and was a little nervous about this gig, so I gave him some pointers backstage before the show. "Just take out any sex jokes, don't swear, and you'll be fine," I told him. He followed my advice, went on, and was killing. Ten minutes into his set, everyone was howling. They were giggling at his setups, roaring at his punch lines. He had them in the palm of his hand. I was loving it. Then he started his next joke: "I was asleep one night, and I heard a loud noise downstairs. I was scared, so I rolled over, tapped my girlfriend, and said, 'Hey, go down there and find out what's going on.'" The room went silent. It stayed silent. He limped through the rest of his set, came offstage, and looked at me, puzzled.

"What happened out there?" he asked me. "It was going so well."

"That joke you told. You can't be in bed with your girlfriend," I told him.

"What do you mean?" he said. "It wasn't about sex."

"Yeah, but unmarried, sleeping together—that's kind of frowned upon. If you're doing it, you're for sure keeping that a secret, not bragging about it, at least around church."

I realize now his flop was sort of my fault. I have so internalized the norms that come along with church that they're second nature to me. I lived my whole life in this bubble. I know exactly where the line is and how far I can go across it before I start getting angry emails. Vinnie was an outsider and needed more instructions than I gave him. But this is another challenge with doing comedy in churches: These are jokes—they're not autobiography, and they're not testimony. We make them up. But church brings with it a set of standards that is alien to most comedians.

It's all about knowing your audience. I have a bit that makes fun of gluten-free communion. I imagined someone dropping dead from the gluten they ingested during communion, then going to heaven and having to explain to everyone up there what happened. Recalling that bit still makes me chuckle, and at most evangelical churches, that joke killed. But when I did it at a Catholic church, the room went silent, because to Catholics, communion is not a symbol; it is considered the actual body of Christ, and I was making it into a joke. In the moment it happened, I instantly related to Vinnie. I was shocked and confused. "Why aren't they laughing?" It wasn't until after the show that the priest explained it all to me, which was nice of him . . . though I still haven't been asked back to that particular church.

This isn't really about religion, per se; it's more about communicating with whatever crowd is in front of you. I know Black comics and Latino comics and Jewish comics and Middle Eastern comics who use all kinds of insider language and cultural references in their bits. If you're not in their demographic, the jokes—if they're good—will still be funny. But if you are in it, you're likely going to be doubled over laughing.

HERE GOES NOTHING

For any kind of comedian, smartphones and social media have changed the rules of engagement entirely. Being a comedian these days is very, very tough. It's always been incredibly hard to make a living telling jokes, but now there is the added challenge of trying to write material and test it out when you've got an audience full of people at a club with their fingers poised to record your joke and share it all over Twitter alongside their overly serious analysis. Next thing you know, you have a social media feed filled with angry @s calling you a sexist, ignorant, insensitive jerk. (Actually, that's the G-rated version of what you'd get called.)

So many comics won't play college campuses anymore because in these so-called safe spaces, the audiences can be hypersensitive about what you can and can't say. But that's just the extreme end of a larger problem that has infected all of comedy. It's a minefield out there. You've got to be very careful where you step . . . or stand, I guess.

If being a comedian today is tough, being a Christian comedian feels like a suicide mission. You get rewarded for going up to the line, but you get *crushed* when you cross it. And the line is different every night! So of course it's going to end poorly. Trying to navigate the Christian community's standards of not just what jokes you can tell but also what kind of role model you have to be in order to tell them, while still trying to make audiences laugh—a camel passing through the eye of a needle would have had an easier time of it. (That's a Matthew 19:24 reference, for those of you keeping score at home.)

If I'm operating by the comedian's moral code, the list of things I'm not supposed to do is pretty short: Don't get too drunk to perform. Don't have sex with the waitstaff. And even those rules are pretty negotiable. Whereas if I'm being judged by the Christian's moral code, the list of things I can't do is basically endless: Don't curse. Don't drink a beer. Don't talk about being in bed with your girlfriend. Don't have sex. Don't talk about sex. Don't even think about sex. Don't go for a jog through your neighborhood on Sunday morning because people will assume you aren't going to church. For real, that's a thing. So, trying to operate on the lonely thin strip of land where these two moral codes intersect is pretty close to impossible. But it's also an imbalance, which is ripe for humor.

I'll go into way more detail about all this later in the book, but in late 2019, I basically got canceled. A story came out about me having inappropriate relationships with women, being dishonest in my personal life, and just generally not living up to the clean-cut, church-friendly image I'd been portraying for years. That's the best way to describe it, I guess. The whole thing really threw my life into disarray and caused me to reexamine a lot of things, including how *and why* I constructed that image in the first place.

To be clear, it's not anyone else's fault that I tried to present myself as this bastion of Christian rectitude. I suppose all the untagging, the deleting, the manicuring of my social media, the flat-out lying, was my way of trying to get everyone to like me, to be accepted, to feel loved. But it was exhausting. You know, I tell a joke that roasts a famous pastor. *I thought John was a Christian.* So I'd tell the joke at my live shows but never post it online for fear of my reputation. Someone posts a photo of me with a girl at a bar in Nashville at midnight on a Tuesday night. *I thought John was a Christian.* It all felt like *a lot.* So I built a house of secrets and then hid out there, hoping no one would ever discover I wasn't the guy I said I was. I know, I know, it's crazy that such a seemingly foolproof strategy didn't work out in the end. Who knew?

5

DO I KNOW YOU?

One of the biggest shows of my life was at the Wiltern theater in late 2018. The Wiltern is a historic Art Deco theater in the heart of Los Angeles. The place is kind of a Hollywood landmark. People like Prince and Lady Gaga have headlined there. It's where Tom Petty recorded a live album. During my 2018 tour, I sold the place out. It was a real rock-star moment for me: big ol' tour bus, my promotional posters tacked up everywhere out front, line around the block. I was feeling pretty good about myself. It was also a homecoming of sorts: I lived in L.A. at the time, and to sell that place out was a real flex.

Anyway, a couple of hours before showtime, I headed to the back door so I could get in and do my sound check. The security woman at the door blocked my way.

"Do you have a pass?" she asked me, stone faced.

I didn't have one. I'd left mine on the bus or something. So I said to her, "Yo, my name is literally on the marquee!"

She was unmoved. "Sorry."

"I don't have an all-access lanyard," I continued, "but my face is actually plastered up all over this building!"

She looked hard at me. She looked at the building. She looked at me again. She shrugged. Long story short, I had to text someone on our crew to let me in.

That's a great depiction of the level of my fame: A lot of people really like me, and a lot of people have no idea who I am. Actually, *most* people have no idea who I am. (Unless, of course, you grew up in the South going to church, in which case your chance of knowing who I am increases tenfold.)

I think about my place in the world of famous people this way. You've got your A-list celebrities: your LeBrons, your T-Swifts, your B-Coops. (That's Bradley Cooper, by the way. I liked the *T-Swift* designation so much that I decided to do the same with Bradley's name. If that catches on because of this book, B-Coops owes me big-time.) And then you've got your B-listers: maybe an NBA player who's not in the starting five, a Real Housewife, a Kardashian cousin, or a guy like Trey Kennedy. (Just kidding, Trey. You're always an A-lister in my heart, bro.) Kathy Griffin had a television show a while back called *My Life on the D-List*. Well, I think I'm less well known than she is, so I guess I'm probably on the E-list.

For most people, the name *John Crist* doesn't mean much. But people see my face and frequently go, "Oh, that guy! He's that guy from that thing I've seen." Often that thing you've seen is a video I posted on the internet. Maybe "Homeschoolers During COVID" or "Every Guy at Home Depot." As of the time I'm writing this, my videos have been watched more than one billion times. I don't mean to brag, but that's a lot of views. I'm not a statistician, but there are only 332 million people in the United States. I'm pretty sure that means that on average, each American has watched at least three of my videos—math don't lie!—though I sometimes fear that the truth is maybe a little closer to three people watching my videos 332 million times each. (Thanks, Aunt Kendra!) Anyway, all that has created a pretty peculiar sort of fame for me.

The last time I was at Disneyland, a woman came up to me and said, "Has anyone ever told you that you look like this comedian?"

I was like, "Who?"

"Oh, I don't know his name," she told me. "He's this Christian comedian. He makes these long, funny Instagram stories."

"Wow, he sounds terrible."

She shrugged her shoulders and continued on her way.

That sort of thing happens all the time. Every time I do a radio interview, I'm like, "Yo, this is pointless. No one knows my voice." But when people *see* me, they're like, "Where do I know this guy from?" One time a lady recognized me and said, "You look familiar. Did you used to be the manager at the Wendy's on West End?" Oookay, lady. Point being, I look kind of familiar. People have seen me on their Instagram feed or when their cousin shared my "Fear Factor in 2021" video on Facebook.

I actually enjoy these sorts of encounters with strangers. I was in a Bed Bath & Beyond not too long ago, and the woman working at the register did the whole "You look familiar" thing. I decided to be straight with this nice lady. I nodded and said something like, "Yeah, I'm a stand-up comedian. Or maybe you've seen one of my viral videos."

She looked at me closely and shook her head. "No, that's not it," she said. "You look like the lead singer of Papa Roach." I don't know what that guy looks like, but I took my receipt and left.

I've gotten kind of used to this now. A few years ago, I was living in an apartment complex that was right next to Belmont University in Nashville, so lots of college kids lived there. When I went to get my mail one day, a cute girl in her twenties immediately came up to me and smiled. "Hey, are you John Crist?"

I puffed out my chest a little and smiled back. "Yep, that's me."

She nodded. "Yeah, my mom loves you."

My chest automatically deflated. Sweet. Yes, moms tend to love me. I don't know why. Moms and Chick-fil-A customers. Those are my key demographics, apparently.

People always know me in Chick-fil-A. Maybe it's because I've made tons of videos about the chain, or maybe it's because they're kind of Christian, or maybe me and my fans just share a taste for high-quality chicken products. Whatever the reason, the place is like a home away from home for me. It's my safe space.

I once told my old road manager Erica the story about a time when I was feeling a little down and insecure about myself, so I went into Chick-fil-A for a quick rush of affirmation. Erica told me, quite sensibly, that it probably wasn't a healthy way to handle my insecurities. I promised her I'd work on it. So every now and then, instead of texting me and asking how I'm doing or what I'm up to, she just says, "You staying out of Chick-fil-A?" The answer to that question is a pretty good indicator of my emotional health at the moment.

It's interesting the places my particular level of fame has currency. I go to an NBA game, and no one knows me. I go to a NASCAR race, and everyone does. It's very strange. And at the beginning of my career, it was a real challenge. For the first six years that I was touring as a stand-up, I traveled alone. I would go onstage and feel like the center of the universe to these crowds: standing ovations, pictures, autographs. Then I'd leave the building, get in my car, and return to being a nobody. The dichotomy of that was shocking, and it led me to some dark places.

Early in my career, I took literally every gig I could. Not because I needed the money—I didn't really care about the money. Still don't, honestly. What I cared about was the affirmation, the love, or whatever form of love I thought I was getting from the stage. I craved that. I had to have it. Out there on the road, I was larger than life. Back at home, I was taking out the trash and picking up the mail like everyone else.

Sometimes I forget my peculiar public profile. When I have a big viral video or a sold-out show or something like that, I can get a big head. I was walking through the airport in Houston once, and there was a family looking at me and pointing. I thought, *Ugh, everywhere I go, people want a selfie. I'll probably have to sign some autographs too.* But I figured I'd be a gracious star and give this family a nice thrill. I went up to them and said something like, "Hey, did you have fun at the show last night?" No lie, the mom said, "We don't know anything about a show, but our daughter thinks you look like Jimmy Neutron." Wow. This really happened. Not only was I not a celebrity to this family, but I was being mistaken for another celebrity who is a children's cartoon character whose run ended in 2006. I've told this story onstage many times, and still to this day people tag me in photos of Jimmy Neutron. Thanks, guys.

On that same tour, I was playing a club called Hilarities in Cleveland. Before my show, I was walking to get something to eat and noticed that at the House of Blues, across the street, there was a line outside going around the block twice. I walked over and asked who was playing. I was told it was Tech N9ne. At the time, I had no idea who or what that was. (I do now: He's a hard-core rapper from Kansas City with a massive cult following.) I love that. I love that pop culture is so big and diverse that a contingent of fans large enough to wrap around a city block is absolutely rabid for someone I've never heard of. And I realize that to them, I'm exactly the same thing. I'm the Tech N9ne of comedy. And you know what? I can live with that.

6

HOMESCHOOLING WAS THE GOODEST

When I was about ten years old, the most fun thing I was allowed to do was ride my bike to the library. That may sound kind of lame, but I swear it wasn't. This was the nineties. We didn't have a TV in my house, we would never have been allowed to have video games, and the internet was but a distant rumor. So my bicycle was everything. Even at age ten, I could cruise around my hometown like I ran the place. Just imagine a scene from *Training Day*—riding bikes through the hood, trying to hide from the cops. It was that, except for the exact opposite. I could hit the park, I could hit the convenience store at the Hess gas station, I could even ride to Chick-fil-A. The library, though, that was the hot spot. It was exactly 1.7 miles away from my house. (I just googled it.) Normally, I'd ride around with my brothers, but for some reason, this one day, I rode my bike alone to the library. I'm sure some helicopter moms out there are freaking out as they read this, but give my parents a break. It was a different time. They had eight kids. Unless you raised eight or more kids on middle-class wages without a steady diet of midafternoon martinis (or something stronger), you don't get to judge.

Anyway, on the day in question, I spent my typical few hours in the library devouring books and then went to the checkout with the ones I'd selected. It was a real Kevin-McCallister-in-*Home-Alone*-at-the-convenience-store type situation. Anyway, I went outside with my yellow backpack full of books, excited to pedal home and ingest my latest finds, when I looked and saw that my bike was not where I had left it. I retraced my steps but still couldn't find it. I wondered if I had misremembered where I parked it. No, it was definitely gone. I hadn't locked it up because no one locked their bikes. This was small town U.S.A. We didn't need locks. We trusted our neighbors. (Again, very much not *Training Day*.) Well, I did until this day. Because outside that library, an alarming and inescapable truth was staring me in the face: My bike had been stolen.

You may think this isn't that big of a deal, but at my age, a bike was all I had! It was my prized possession. It gave me freedom and independence. Without it, how was I going to get around? My parents couldn't shuttle all eight of us wherever we needed to go. There was no Uber. Without my bike, I was half a man, er, half a boy. But my more immediate problem was how to get back to my house. There were no cellphones back then to call home and ask for a ride. I wasn't gonna hitchhike. So I did the only thing I could: I walked home (1.7 miles) with a backpack full of books, dejected and crying.

By the time I finally got home, it was dark. All my family was inside eating dinner. I walked through the back door crying and told them about the horrific crime that had been done to me. I explained that my bike was gone, stolen, snatched. As much as I'm joking about it now, it was genuinely traumatic. My family's reaction ranged from indifference to ridicule. My older brothers immediately started making fun of me. All I needed at the time was a little compassion—for someone to tell me that it was a horrible thing to have happen and that they'd help me find the culprits who took it. But no one did.

To be clear, that's how *I* remember the story happening. Ask my older brothers and they'd probably have no recollection of this whatsoever. It was not a formative event for them. And I'm sure if my parents knew the seriousness of what had happened, they'd have immediately sprang into action. But childhood trauma works like that, doesn't it? You remember the *very* specifics of events like that. I can remember it all like it were yesterday: my yellow backpack, my Dyno bike, the long teary walk home. I remember it all.

In fact, if you've ever seen a video I've shot at my house, you may have noticed a bike chandelier in my dining room. A girl I dated was so moved by that story that she got on eBay and found the exact bike—color, wheels, everything—and had that chandelier made. It's legit my favorite thing in my house. When we broke up, she gave me my hoodies back, and the photo of her on the car dashboard had to go, but I kept the chandelier. That's an amazing piece of sentimental art. Plus, it would have been way more awkward to return it to her.

LIVING IN A BUBBLE

I grew up in a beautiful old white Victorian house in Lilburn, Georgia. In many ways, it was idyllic. There was a wide front porch and a big yard in back, and it was ringed by an actual white picket fence. Across the street was a public park, where

I'd play basketball and tennis, and there was a Chick-fil-A less than a mile away that, as I mentioned, I could ride my bike to. I actually worked there in high school.

The house I grew up in had once been a train station, and people were constantly stopping by to see it or to visit my father, who was a pastor at a prominent local church and a well-known figure in the community. Our house even had—and still has—a big white sign out front with the words "The Crist House" emblazoned on it, which seems to mark it as some sort of small-town tourist attraction. All this added up to us often feeling like we were on display, like everyone was looking at us—this big family with eight kids, homeschooled, well-known father, in a house that looked like a museum right in the center of town. It was as if we were living in a snow globe. My life was right out there, literally on Main Street, for all the world to see, from day one. In hindsight, probably no one cared all that much, but that's what it *felt* like.

My parents were strict with us. We had manners. Lots of rules. We were taught to say *please* and *thank you, sir* and *ma'am*. We always stood up straight. Posture was a big issue in the Crist family. I remember being constantly reminded to sit up straight.

When we were kids, the absolute worst thing you could do was embarrass the family. Keeping up appearances was of the utmost importance. The Crist family was into the idea of getting likes way before social media even existed. One time my dad was giving a sermon and heard a bunch of kids running around on the roof of the church. He detoured from his sermon to bemoan the clattering and misbehavior going on above him. "Can you believe parents these days?" he asked the congregation. "Some don't seem to know how to discipline their children." Maybe you can tell where this story is going: Yes, it was me on the roof of the church, playing freeze tag with my buddy Robby. When my dad found this out, I got spanked harder than I'd ever been spanked in my life. I know many parents are anti-spanking, but I probably had that one coming.

That's how discipline was generally meted out in the Crist family. Whatever the misdeed, the punishment often came in the shape of the wooden paddle my dad used to spank us. To be fair, there were eight of us kids, all two years apart, and there really wasn't time for nurturing lessons about why we don't do this or why we don't do that. (Or maybe we did have those nurturing lessons, but it probably tells you all you need to know that I have no real recollection of them. The spankings I remember.) Pushing my brother off his seat at dinner—that was worth a spanking. Failing to come into the house when my mom whistled for me—I swear I didn't hear her!—that's a spanking. Playing freeze tag on the roof of the church during dad's sermon—definitely a spanking. There were even group spankings. My brother farted in church. We both got spanked.

"Why am I getting spanked for this?" I asked.

"You laughed. You encouraged it."

My dad's spanking paddle, by the way, was something to behold: It was about sixteen inches long and an inch thick, with a handle at the bottom. He'd carved it himself from wood and drilled holes in it, I suppose to make it more aerodynamic or maybe to make it hurt that much more when it hit our bare skin. He actually broke that paddle on one of my brothers eventually, but the remnants of it are still at my parents' house to this day. It's really just a wooden handle and some splintered wood now. I apologize if this has triggered traumatic memories of your own childhood spankings, though as much as mine hurt at the time, all these years later, most of those memories just make me laugh.

There were occasionally other, more creative, punishments. I remember once calling my brother a fool. This was treated as a grave transgression. There's a Bible verse—Matthew 5:22—that says that if you call your brother a fool, you're in danger of hell's fire. My parents took this 100 percent literally. I got my mouth washed out with soap for it. My mom took an actual bar of soap and rubbed it on my tongue. It's crazy. I know it sounds like I'm telling stories from the 1800s or something, but this was the 1990s!

Then there was the time I stole Laffy Taffy from the Hess station near our house. I couldn't have been more than eleven years old. I rode my bike there to buy a Little Debbie Oatmeal Creme Pie for twenty-five cents. Laffy Taffy probably cost a nickel, and I had enough money for it, but for some reason— maybe just because I knew it was wrong—I took the candy and walked out. I got home and shoved this purple Laffy Taffy under my pillow. My mom found it and confronted me. There were a million possible and completely plausible explanations for where I could've gotten this candy—for example, from one of my brothers, from a kid at the park across the street. But I wasn't a seasoned liar, and she could read it all over my face. I broke down immediately, sobbing, and admitted I'd stolen it from the Hess station. My dad put me in the car, drove us to the station, and walked me inside, straight to the register.

"This is my son John, and he has something he'd like to say to you."

At this point, I was already crying, snot running down my face. "I stole this Laffy Taffy," I blubbered. "I'll never do it again. I'm sorry for stealing it."

Keep in mind, the kid working the register was probably making minimum wage, was very possibly stoned, and was in any case completely ill-equipped and utterly disinterested in playing a part in the ethical melodrama being performed in front of him. He couldn't have cared less. He just shrugged, took back the Laffy Taffy, and put it back on the shelf. Apparently, you could just do that back then.

THOSE WERE THE DAYS

I know it sounds like I'm complaining about this rough, awful childhood, but I swear I'm not. I look back on the way I grew up and think it was actually pretty awesome. Yes, it was strict, and yes, I got spanked with a paddle, and yes, I had my mouth washed out with soap, and yes, we didn't have a TV, but I spent hours upon hours outside at the park, playing in the woods, building forts, and riding bikes with my brothers.

My siblings and I were all homeschooled when we were younger. The public schools were considered worldly. They taught evolution, and that was a problem in The Crist House. We were taught to fear public school. Once when I was acting up, my dad actually threatened me by saying, "Don't make me send you to public school." I broke down in tears. Really.

Our homeschooling textbooks were all Christian. They taught principles from the Bible. Even the math was biblical. We'd read the parable of the rich young ruler from Matthew 19:16–30 and then have to answer questions like "If the rich young man had 10 shekels and lost 50 percent of his investment, how many shekels did he have left?" (See answer key at the back of this book.)

There are many stereotypes about homeschooled kids, and while we undoubtedly fit some of them, my parents did everything they could to make sure our lives weren't completely sheltered. They insisted that we mixed with other kids. We all had to take art classes, go to piano lessons, and play sports. After a couple of years, everyone sort of found their niche. I loved sports and played in a basketball league that was specifically for homeschooled kids. It was quite the scene. We had to wear long pants because shorts were considered immodest. The girls' team had to wear these crazy culottes, which are basically wide, calf-length pants, sort of like the world's most ill-fitting, unfashionable capris. They looked like something you'd see on an Amish farm.

As a pastor, my dad was funny and charismatic, and I guess I must have inherited some of that from him. Not to brag, but I was suuuuuper-popular around my church. People always seemed interested in whatever I was doing. I had lots of friends. I think my father must have seen that performer's spark in me, because when I graduated from college, he asked me if I wanted to take over the church from him one day. Not that being a pastor is the exact same as being a performer, but you get the idea. He wanted me to be the next pastor. I didn't want to do it. I knew even back then that that life wasn't for me.

As you can imagine, a family of eight kids, all being homeschooled, made our house a scene of barely controlled chaos on a daily basis. My mom was in charge of waking us up every morning, feeding us, getting us all to our various basketball practices, painting classes, and piano lessons, and then on top of all that, being our schoolteacher. To say it was a lot for her is a grand understatement. After my youngest sister, Evangeline, was born, my mom was kinda maxed out. She was physically and emotionally exhausted. Looking back on it now, it's shocking that she didn't reach her breaking point any sooner than that. Once, I babysat my nephew for two hours while my brother and sister-in-law went to dinner. I was exhausted when they finally got back. I was watching one kid. For two hours. My mom had eight kids, aged zero to sixteen, and she was dutifully doing *everything* for all of them, all the time. At a certain point, that's just not sustainable anymore. She fell pretty deep into postpartum depression.

THE STREETS (OF LILBURN)

Life had to change for us. A nanny was hired. This other lady came in once a week just to do the laundry. But the biggest change is that once we were old enough, we started attending a private Christian school, Providence Christian Academy. I was in eighth grade then, and it was eye opening. This wasn't the mean streets of Compton by any stretch of the imagination, but it was a different world.

Despite the fact that I was a skinny, four-feet-eleven homeschooler, I was an oddly cocky kid at that point in my life. (As an adult, I could tell you that the cockiness was a coping mechanism to cover insecurity, but I just learned that, like, three weeks ago.) My dad was the pastor, and I was used to being a kind of VIP in the small universe around my church. At Providence, I got bullied a bit, though maybe I had it coming. I remember at lunch my first year there, I playfully swiped some food off a kid's tray in the cafeteria, and he threw me under the table and kicked me. I wasn't seriously injured, but it hit me at that moment, *Oh, these people are not my friends.*

I tried to make adjustments. When I was in eighth grade, I had to give a report about my interests to my English class. It's almost crazy how clearly I can remember this: There I was, standing in front of the class, whiteboard behind me, Mrs. Tester's desk to my right, and the large glass windows at the back of the classroom looking out onto the parking lot. At the time, I was really into this Christian rock band DC Talk, but when I got to the line in the report where I had written, "I love riding bikes, and my favorite band is DC Talk," I quickly subbed in *No Doubt* for *DC Talk*. Even though this was a Christian school, I somehow intuited that these kids weren't like me. They hadn't been homeschooled, and a Christian band like DC Talk would definitely not have been considered cool. So it was already my reflex, even at age thirteen, to hide that part of myself that I thought people wouldn't accept.

Before I even went to Providence, my mom took me across town one day to sit in a little room and take a standardized placement test. Because I'd been homeschooled, they had to figure out what grade level I was at academically. Now, I'll be honest: When we were being homeschooled, I was not a good student. My brothers were motivated and would finish their assignments easily. I always had something else I'd rather be doing. I was easily distracted and required a little more attention before I'd buckle down and get my work done.

I'm not sure exactly how I did on this placement test, but when I got my schedule on my first day at Providence, it looked pretty much like everyone else's—you know, first period English, second period math, third period history, and so on—except for my sixth-period class. For sixth period, I had to leave the high school wing of the building, walk over to the elementary school wing, and go into a smaller classroom with only about six desks. Instead of there being one teacher for fifteen or twenty kids, there was one teacher for every kid. I was thirteen at the time, and most of the other kids in the class with me were nine or ten. Something was wrong here.

The work we were asked to do was odd too. There were lots of memory-type games. We'd be asked to look at three shapes and then decide which one we saw first. Or there would be a group of objects and we had to pick the one that didn't belong. When we did something well, we got to put a little star sticker by our name on a poster board. It was *real* basic. My brother was in AP literature, and I was practically playing with blocks.

I asked some of the other kids in my grade if they had that class too, but none of them did. In fact, they had never heard of it and didn't even know the part of the school where it was. At that age, no one wants to be different, and because nobody was telling me anything about what this class was all about, I was confused. I went home and told my parents that there had been some kind of mistake. I needed to switch out of that class. They made it clear that this class was not optional.

So I kept going. After a while, it dawned on me that that sixth-period class was for people with learning disabilities. And I was in this class. Which—by the transitive property that I'm sure I didn't understand at that point in my life—meant, in turn, that I *had* a learning disability. Only nobody ever told me I had one. So almost immediately I felt bad about it. I felt shame. I tried my best to hide it. After fifth period, I would kind of slink out the door and sneak up to this class, hoping that none of my friends saw me and asked where I was going. I may have had a learning disability, but it didn't take me long to learn that a learning disability was something to hide.

My parents were great about celebrating their kids' accomplishments. When my brother made the honor roll, we had a little family party. When my other brother made the basketball team, same deal. I had to take that sixth-period class for two semesters before I "graduated" from it. But there was no party for that. No one ever mentioned it. I can look back on it now and understand that my parents probably felt like drawing more attention to it might embarrass me, but not talking about it at all and not acknowledging that this learning disability was part of who I was made it really hard to be proud of who I was. I was already beginning to understand that there was a difference between the person you really are and the person you show to the world.

Providence was the first time being around people I knew didn't like me. For someone who was forever searching out affirmation and approval, it was pretty jarring. I'd get called names and occasionally pushed into a locker, but this was a small Christian private school, so it's not as if there were knife fights in the hallways or anything. One time I did get bullied pretty hard by a kid named Kyle. (Okay, his name is not really Kyle. But if I include his real name, the book publisher is going to make me find him on Facebook, message him, and get him to sign a release saying he won't sue me for calling him a bully, and I really don't want to do that. I know confronting our bullies is supposed to be some sort of liberating exercise, but tracking this dude down all these years later feels more silly than liberating.

So for the purposes of this story, he's just Kyle.) Anyway, Kyle threw me on top of some lockers in the locker room before basketball practice. I then fell from this perch, six feet or so off the ground, but landed on an open locker on the way down. I still have a scar on my upper thigh from it. I had to limp out to practice with blood dripping from my shorts.

The injury wasn't that serious, but what I remember most about that experience is the feeling that nobody really noticed other than me. Here I was, a fourteen-year-old kid, bleeding throughout a two-hour basketball practice, and the coach never said anything, and neither did my teammates. You'd think at the very least the janitorial staff would be a little dismayed to see some kid dripping blood all over the nice gym floor, but no. Nobody seemed to care. I got home, and it was more of the same. I told my mom I was bleeding, and she told me to take a shower. *What?* I'd like to think this was a parenting strategy intent on toughening me up, making me self-sufficient, but the truth is a lot less heady. Mom had seven other kids to look after, dinner to make, laundry to do, and homework to check. A cut on my leg didn't change any of that. It was sort of like the stolen-bike episode all over again.

I often felt like I got lost in the shuffle growing up. I played tennis back then and was pretty serious about it. I used to have practice every day from three-thirty to five-thirty at the courts about twenty minutes from my house. Most of the other kids' parents would turn up to pick their kids up around five-fifteen so they could watch the last few minutes of practice and then maybe talk to the coach for a minute. At five-thirty, everyone would start filing out. My parents wouldn't be there yet. At five-forty-five, still no word from them. Six o'clock, nothing.

My coach couldn't just leave a thirteen-year-old kid by himself, so he would have to sit there with me outside the tennis center, growing gradually more and more pissed off. Again, this was the era before everyone had cellphones. So I'd sit there with my water bottle and tennis racket, trying not to cry, and hoping to God that my parents' car would be the next one to come around the corner.

I know in the scheme of great childhood traumas, it doesn't seem that bad—and it wasn't—but this kind of stuff left a mark on me. It formed the person I became. I don't blame my parents, really. There were just so many of us kids, and there were only so many hours in the day that my parents could pay attention to us, particularly my dad, who spent a lot of time working. It seemed like he was always at the church, on his way to the church, or too busy to throw a football in the yard because he had to get to the church. We all were involved at church—one of my brothers was on the worship team, two of them played in the band, my mom played violin, and my sister worked in the nursery—but my dad always seemed to have ten other things he needed to be doing when we were there.

I was desperate for my father's attention in any way I could get it. I remember my mom telling me once that he was going to be at one of my tennis matches. I was thrilled. But when the match started, I looked out into the bleachers and he wasn't there. Thirty minutes in, still no dad. I was a good little tennis player, but I started losing the match intentionally to drag it out in hopes that my father would show up. When he finally did, I was down big and then mounted what must have seemed like an incredible miracle comeback, winning in three sets. It wasn't even as planned out as I'm making it sound. It just kind of happened. On some level, a part of my brain kicked in and was like, *Here's a good idea: Start losing and when your dad shows up, you can come back and WIN. He'll be so proud.* It's crazy how my middle school brain was longing for something before I could even articulate it and that it was able to concoct a rather elaborate ruse to fulfill that need. It would not be the last time my brain did something like that.

7

SAME PHONE. WHO DIS?

I talk a lot onstage about being human. Like, I want to think I'm a good person, but the reality is, I'm probably not. I got a new phone not too long ago and was adjusting all the settings and stuff like that. Do I want ESPN notifications on for scores and updates? Yes, I do. Do I want Amber Alerts on for missing children? Naaaaaaaah, I'm good. That's how nice of a guy I *really* am. Okay, come on, don't tell me you haven't thought about turning those off too. Recently, onstage, I'm pretty sure the words "I love Jesus, but I hate some people" came out of my mouth. So, yeah, I've got some issues. I often marvel at the people who run marathons or spend their Saturdays volunteering for Habitat for Humanity. I'm like, *Who are these alien creatures?*

One time onstage, I asked this guy in the front row if he thought he was a good person. "Sure," he said, not thinking twice. "Okay," I replied, "unlock your phone and hand it up to me. We'll see." Not surprisingly, he recoiled in fear. We all like to think we're good people, the heroes of our own story. But no one wants a stranger scrolling through their phone, because in this day and age, scrolling through someone's phone is about as close as you can get to rummaging through the back alleys of their mind. Shoot, I don't want anyone going through mine! The profiles I've looked at, the screenshots I've taken, the texts I've sent to my group chat with my three best friends from high school—that's all in there.

The crazy thing is, your apps already know. Whatever bands I tell people I'm into, Spotify knows better. That's why it keeps feeding me Kenny Chesney! I have the Bible app on my phone. On page one. I remember opening it to look up a verse that I was thinking about and a notification popped up that said, "You have not opened this app in over a year. A new version is available. You are a terrible person." Kidding about the "terrible person" part. That was just going on in my head.

And what about your phone's internal GPS? For the most part, I'm down with people knowing where I am, but I remember going on a family vacation once and my cousin suggesting we all turn on location sharing so we could always find one another. I was like, *Okay, slow down with that idea, bro.*

I used to think way more than I should about what I chose to like on social media. Has anyone else done this? For example, a buddy of mine posted a photo at a Nashville Predators hockey game. I liked it. The next day, he posted a photo of him hunting quail. I didn't like that one. I personally don't have much of an issue with hunting, but I didn't want to be perceived as some kind of anti-animal or pro-gun guy. Not that I need to profess my stance on either, but I just didn't want to be *perceived* as one or the other on the internet.

I try my best to curate my Instagram account to make myself seem like a good person. I like things that I'm proud to put my name on. But my Instagram Explore page—that's a different story. The Explore page will take you into a world that is more authentically *you* than you may be comfortable with. These pages are created based not on what you like or who you follow but rather what you click on and what you look at in the app. Yikes, I know. Let me look at mine right now. A lot of it is the NBA, golf, and NASCAR. PR-wise, it would be better if there were some WNBA sprinkled in there, but here we are. There's a Kristin Cavallari bikini photo—I'm sure because she lives in Nashville and the algorithm knows we have mutual friends, not because I have maybe scrolled through her feed a few times. At least that's what I tell myself.

But the part of your phone that probably knows you best is your battery. Go to your phone's settings and click on your battery. Most smartphones will display which apps you're expending the most battery power on. I can have the Bible app, a couple of fitness apps, and Audible all displayed prominently on my phone's front page, but my battery knows I spend a lot more time on Reddit, dating apps, and TikTok than reading Corinthians, working out, and listening to audiobooks.

QUEUE VERSUS YOU

Data collection and privacy are big issues right now, and there are certainly ways of keeping your phone from knowing so much about you. But for most of us, the convenience of opening up Apple Maps and being immediately able to click on our home address (as opposed to typing it in every time) easily outweighs the small chance that anyone will ever find out (or really care) that your most frequented address is Taco Bell. The price of that convenience is that the real you, warts and all, is right there inside your phone or on your laptop or even on your TV.

And, at times, it's leaking out. You may bookmark the *Wall Street Journal,* Charity Navigator, and Crosswalk.com on your laptop, but your internet-browser history tells us that you've actually spent most of your time online playing poker, watching "Fail!" videos on YouTube, and checking your fantasy-football lineup. That's you. It's who you are.

Netflix does the same thing. A few years ago, I went on a date with a girl and invited her over to watch a movie. I pulled up my Netflix to browse through some options and choose a movie for us. As I was scrolling through, the "Continue Watching" section came up. It listed *New Girl, Trailer Park Boys, Superbad,* and *The Secret Life of Pets 2.* Listen, draw whatever conclusions you'd like from that, but that's an uncomfortable thing for a woman who I was on a first date with to know, right? But now that I know this section will likely appear, sometimes I'll start stuff on Netflix just so it populates my "Continue Watching." That way, if a girl is coming over, she can see the person I want her to think I am. Okay, I know, I'm the worst. But you've got to admit that even if you've never done the exact same thing, right now you're thinking about trying it.

It's like this: My Netflix queue is filled with probing, artful shows and movies that have often come highly recommended from people whose opinions I really trust: *The Crown, Lupin, Black Mirror, 13th, Peaky Blinders, Seaspiracy, When They See Us.* I have every intention of watching each of these. One day. But *today,* I can guarantee you, when I open up Netflix, I'm going to watch *Outer Banks.* Again. (But only because *The Office* is no longer on Netflix.) My Netflix queue is my best version of myself. It's the me I really want to be but rarely am. The cool me.

The smart me. The righteous me. On the other hand, if you explore my Netflix *history,* that's the real me.

Your Netflix queue is almost like a postmodern version of a bookshelf. (And make no mistake, *my* book better be at eye level on the bookshelf in your house. Or better yet, on the coffee table. If I have to crouch down to read the spine of it, I'm leaving immediately.) For my parents' generation, your bookshelves were the way you showed off your intellectual chops to all your visitors and flexed the broad range of things you were interested in. And the fact that you had barely cracked the spine on most of those books was a secret that you could generally keep to yourself. No one had to know that you'd never read *The Grapes of Wrath* or *The Decline and Fall of the Roman Empire* or *The Purpose-Driven Life.* They just had to know you were the *kind* of person who would read those books. Hypothetically. But now technology is outing us. It's showing everyone what we really "read."

RISE OF THE MACHINES

When I was about twenty-five, I was living in Colorado Springs and volunteering heavily at my church. We were big on shame at this church in those days. And there was nothing worse in our minds than porn. We were always hearing sermons about it. We'd be in all types of confessional groups about porn. It was wild.

One day our Bible-study leader came in with an announcement: He'd heard about this app that we could put on our phones that would track *all* our activity. Literally everything— websites, images, texts—that appeared on the screen was logged, and a report was sent to the person of your choice. This was how we were going to stop watching porn or anything else we shouldn't be looking at. For some reason, we thought this was a good idea. We all signed up for the site, listed each other's email addresses, and had someone else set our passwords. So from then on, my internet history was being reported to these friends, and theirs to me. No lie, this is a real thing.

Many parents, I'm sure, are nodding in recognition, knowing they have these types of filters on their children's phones and computers. And to be honest, it *did* kinda help me. Knowing someone else was seeing my browser history made me think twice about the links I was clicking, but it didn't do much of anything to extinguish the impulse driving those clicks. I always *wanted* to look but was scared someone was watching.

I'm not a therapist, but I'm pretty sure that's not the way to change behavior for the long term. I *do* remember once getting a report from my buddy about him looking up massages at 2:00 A.M. I asked him about it. He said he'd been working out and had some back pain. Lol. I didn't know girls in bikinis were the most qualified to help with sports-related injuries, dude. But, hey, I'm not judging. (Okay, maybe a little.)

ICUP

I read a statistic once that public pools are 41 percent urine. Just kidding. I didn't actually read that. I made that up. But it's probably not that far off. My point is, *everybody* pees in the pool. It's a fact of life. If you're hanging out at a pool party with a drink in your hand, talking to a half-dozen people doing the same thing, I can just about guarantee at least one of them is peeing as you're talking. I mean, a dozen people are lying outside by the pool, drinking for four hours, and no one is going inside to pee? Where do you think all that liquid is going? But no one will own up to this. Yet technology is starting to show us the truth. I read about this dye that they can put in pools that reacts with urine to change the color of the water. (I didn't make that up. That one's real.) What that means for all of us is clear: No more pool peeing in peace. The hope is obviously that people, fearing public shame, will start getting out of the pool to use the bathroom. Is this a good thing? For those of us who would rather not be swimming in urine, yes, I suppose it is. But there's a small part of me that wishes we could all just accept the truth about who we really are: people who pee in pools.

The architecture of technology that we've created around our lives has changed the way we think about truth. I mean, is not getting out of the pool to pee the same as lying about it? Is your Netflix queue a lie? What about your Tinder profile? What about that cute photo you posted on Facebook that shows you, your husband, and your kids snuggled up watching TV but fails to mention that ten minutes after that picture was taken, you were still arguing about what to watch?

Recently, I saw a gray hair. On my head. And it was not alone. There were a few of them clustered together, like they were having a meeting, maybe hatching a plan for taking over the rest of my head. A brief wave of panic came over me. I wish I could tell you I was overwhelmed by a reminder of my own mortality or worried about the passage of time or whether I was making the most of my limited days on this earth, but that ain't true. In reality, I was mostly worried about how it would look on social media. Should I now frame myself in Instagram stories from only the right side? What if I got an entirely new haircut so my grays didn't really show anymore? Should I wear a hat everywhere I go from now on? Shave my head bald? Or I could turn to technology—albeit 1980s technology—and head down to CVS to pick up some Just For Men and wash that gray right out of my hair. Then it struck me that there is also another revolutionary option: Just leave it alone and accept that gray hair is part of who I am now. That I, like everyone else on this planet, am getting older and that the physical manifestations of that process are nothing to hide or be ashamed of. That we all need to start to see aging and the wisdom that it brings as a gift and not a curse. But then I discovered this great Instagram filter that I started using on my photos instead!

MARCH OF THE HUMANS

If technology has made it harder to lie to ourselves about who we are, it has also forced us to be accountable for who we claim to be. Back in 2014, Baltimore Ravens running back Ray Rice was arrested for domestic abuse of his then fiancée in a Las Vegas hotel. The NFL suspended Rice for the first two games of the season, but to most fans, this event was simply the latest in a long string of stories about football players mistreating women. Frankly, not that many people really even noticed. At first.

Then technology stepped in. *TMZ* got hold of a disturbing video from the hotel elevator that showed Rice punching his fiancée in the face and then dragging her limp body out of the elevator. It was awful. I remember watching it and being shocked, although I had already read an article spelling out exactly the same thing and not felt the same pang. Immediately, there was a public outcry. The NFL extended his suspension indefinitely, effectively ending his career. But what had changed? The crime was the same, but that video made us all see

how ugly the crime really looked. Technology was not just outing Rice as a criminal; it was outing the NFL and many of its
fans—all of us—as people who stand against this kind of thing
only when we see the evidence with our own eyes. It was putting the truth right in front of our faces: that Ray Rice might
be very good at playing football, but when it came to other
human interactions (like, say, having relationships or riding an
elevator) he was maybe not so good.

Remember when recordings surfaced of the L.A. Clippers'
then owner Donald Sterling making racist statements that same
year? The NBA forced him out. All good, right? But what if the
woman who leaked that audio of Sterling didn't have recordings? What if she had just told some reporter that Sterling was
saying racist stuff? Would anyone have batted an eye? I doubt it.
Because plenty of people had already told reporters that Sterling was a racist. Blake Griffin, a star for the Clippers at the
time, said that when he was drafted by them, he googled Sterling's name and immediately found articles about him being a
racist. But it wasn't until these recordings put his racism in our
ears, on our Twitter feeds, that we were faced with the real
truth and had to deal with it.

The internet has helped us become aware of some massive
wrongdoings in our time, injustices that merit responses. But
there's another layer of internet controversies that is tough to
keep track of. It makes me wonder what it actually means to be
a "responsible consumer" in the internet age. I mean, I now
know Uber doesn't pay their drivers enough or offer them benefits, but does that mean I have to stand on the corner waving
my arm for a taxi like a freakin' caveman? Not to mention, those
drivers are counting on us using that rideshare service to make a

living. When the Papa John's founder uses the N-word on a conference call, we can all agree that's a huge problem, but does it mean I definitely, absolutely, positively can't order the $8.99 large two-topping pizza? Because that's a pretty sick deal. And I'm guessing the pizza-delivery people are still counting on our tips to make ends meet, right? Jeff Bezos may have had an affair when he was married and may not like to pay taxes, but why should that mean I have to drag myself around to four different stores to try to find the kind of moisturizer I like rather than just buying it with 1-Click on Amazon? So if the CEO of a company that sells black beans doesn't vote the way I vote, I've got to start buying beans that I like less and cost more? Am I really supposed to keep track of the private lives and political opinions of all the C-suite executives for any products I buy now?

What I've begun to realize is that for all our howling about boycotting companies and canceling people, if you've got a good product, you've got a lot more leeway. People have been hollering for years about Chick-fil-A's CEO being homophobic, yet every Chick-fil-A drive-through is jammed all the time, and not just in the conservative parts of America. When I lived in L.A., I used to go to one on Hollywood Boulevard, and I can promise you that most of the people in there would loudly trumpet their support for LGBTQ rights and gender equality, but after one bite of that chicken sandwich, they were doing the mental gymnastics to make their lunch morally defensible in their minds.

And what about Subway? Their famous pitchman, seen in commercials for years, was a pedophile who was eventually convicted of some truly disturbing crimes. People were horrified. Yet it's still the biggest fast-food chain in the whole entire world. Because, well, where else are you going to get a foot-long meatball sub toasted with provolone for just five bucks, right?

For all the noise that so-called cancel culture makes, it is not so strong on the follow-through. Remember a few years ago when United Airlines literally dragged that poor dude off one of their planes because he wouldn't get out of his overbooked seat? I mean, they brutalized this guy—a doctor, no less—bloodied him, broke his nose, and knocked out two of his teeth, and the whole thing was recorded by other passengers on their cellphones. Those videos immediately went viral, and we were all lighting United up on Twitter, promising never to fly the airline (the #BoycottUnited hashtag was shared 3.5 million times in the coming days) and sarcastically pitching the company some new ad slogans. (My favorite: "United Airlines. Putting the hospital in hospitality.") Funny thing happened though: In the quarter that followed the incident, United's business actually *improved*. Their revenue was up 6 percent, their profits were up almost 50 percent, and they had more passengers than the same stretch of time the previous year.

How could this happen, you say? Sure, the company did its best to put a PR Band-Aid on the whole thing, but mostly we all rethought our boycott threats when faced with forgoing a $99 direct flight from Chicago to Denver in favor of paying three times as much for a flight that was going to route us through Charlotte and then require a change of planes in St. Louis with only our sparkling virtue to keep us company. Suddenly we started to think, *Hey, that guy could've just cooperated, taken the travel vouchers, and walked off that flight,* or, *I'm sure he instigated the whole thing by trying to bring an extra carry-on bag!*

Of course, none of that outrage would ever have been stoked in the first place without social media. It is an unqualified positive that social media has given every consumer a chance to fight back against corporate behemoths in the court of public opinion, but too often I feel like every time someone overcooks their Big Mac, people run to Twitter or Instagram in the hopes of scoring some internet clout. I mean, think about how many times something like this has popped up in your feed: "Southwest Airlines is horrible. We were delayed OVER AN HOUR, and I missed my sister's dog-adoption ceremony. I will never fly Southwest again and I encourage all of my 117 followers to do the same. #cancelsouthwest." Just once, I'd like to see Southwest clap back. Like, we'd be readying for takeoff and the pilot comes on over the intercom to say, "Judy Carlson, please press your flight-attendant call button. We read your tweet about us, and as a result, you will be on snack duty this entire flight. We're literally flying you across the country for $79, you egomaniacal narcissist. Chill out." Okay, that's probably not going to happen, but I'm holding out hope.

I guess I'm just wondering if we should maybe check our collective outrage so that when we decide to unleash it, it will actually have some meaning. Before social media, an oil company had to destroy the entire coast of Alaska before people would even consider driving an extra block to fill up their gas tank somewhere else. Now if the CEO is caught on camera buying the wrong kind of tuna fish, the pummeling the company will take online will be relentless. Look, I genuinely admire people who feel so strongly about this stuff that they are willing to rearrange their entire existence around every revelation, but I just worry that after I boycott all the companies and CEOs who I don't totally agree with, I may have to live without food, clothing, transportation, entertainment, or sports teams to root for.

In the meantime, Go Washington Football Team!

8

AM I THE ONLY ONE WHO SEES THIS?

I remember exactly where I was when my first video went viral. Or at least as viral as I could go at that time. It's one of those frozen-in-time moments. I was in Tucson, Arizona, working at a comedy club. The day before, I had released a video titled "Christian Girl Instagram." I walked out of my motel room on the second floor, and my friend Kate texted me and said she'd seen my video on one of her friend's pages. This was significant because I didn't know this friend of hers. At the beginning of my career, all the re-shares came from friends and family, but now a *stranger* had shared my video. And then more and more and more strangers did the same. I remember my family buzzing the group text all day: One thousand views, two thousand, ten thousand, one hundred thousand! I was in the clouds! I could've gotten robbed, could've been diagnosed with a deadly disease, and I would not have cared one bit that day. I was on top of the actual world.

The premise of that video was pretty simple. It was a fake infomercial for a book offering "101 Tips & Tricks to Get More Likes on Your Devotional Photos." Many of the jokes were very Christian insider, and you really had to understand that culture to get them, with references to purity rings, specific Bible verses, and Christian authors like Joyce Meyer and Joel Osteen.

But the overall vibe that the video was sending up rang true. So many people had scrolled through Instagram and seen exactly the kind of photos I was talking about: an open Bible with the relevant passage highlighted, next to a bowl of fresh fruit and a coffee mug, outside on the porch on a beautiful morning. These photos looked so ornately crafted, and the point of them was never actually the Bible verse being highlighted; it was trying to convince the internet you're a better Christian than you really are. I mean, just out of frame, I'm sure, is the half-empty bag of Doritos, the pile of dirty laundry on the floor, and the *Us Weekly* with the salsa stain on the cover. Somehow those items don't make it into the photo. I felt like I was witnessing things online that looked so glaringly hypocritical that I'd always just think, *Am I the only one who sees this?* while, of course, ignoring the plank in my own eye. (Again, more on that later.)

What made "Christian Girl Instagram" work as an internet video is the same thing that makes any of my videos work: *truth*. Despite the cultural suggestions, despite whatever they yell on CNN, despite what that angry mob on Twitter is trying to scream at you all day, the truth is what prevails. Always. It's got to be cloaked in humor, but the best and most viral videos are the ones people watch and think, *Oh my goodness. That is so true.*

Most good jokes—video or not—need to tap into the audience's subconscious a little, to say something that everyone knows is true but no one is saying. The social media grandstanding in those Instagram devotional photos was ripe for skewering. Imagine you wake up a little hungover, there's a pizza box on your bed from the night before, and you roll over, unlock your phone, open Instagram, and the first thing you see is a photo of this beautiful person with an open Bible, a highlighter, and a healthy breakfast, with the hashtag #blessed. Imagine how far back in your head your eyes would roll, *especially* if you knew that person and you knew she was tipsy, singing "Friends in Low Places" at the top of her lungs the night before.

As big of a deal as it was for "Christian Girl Instagram" to go viral, what happened after it did was maybe even more impactful in the long run: The day after the video blew up was the first time someone ever publicly criticized me. It was equally surreal. Someone reposted my video and called me sexist, misogynistic, and unchristian. I thought it was a joke. I thought it was another comedian doubling down on my point or something, making fun of people who were offended. But it wasn't. It was a sincere person with a sincere tweet. So I fired back immediately, making fun of them. I had to defend myself! Then my buddies joined in, and it was a whole Twitter mess. People digging up stuff from people's past, trying to shame them. A whole ordeal. That was the first and last time I ever engaged a critic online.

That whole mess sent me into a creative spiral. I didn't post another video for at least six months. I felt paralyzed. I had wanted attention so badly, but once there were people outside my circle, who didn't know me in real life, watching my videos, they were going to interpret the jokes in their own way. And though it took me some time to understand this, I totally get why people were upset by that video. I don't think that I'm sexist or misogynistic, and I don't think that video is either, but it took aim at something that was extremely intimate and personal. I was making fun of how someone reads the Bible. But if you are someone who spent two minutes reading a passage from Luke and then thirty-five minutes staging and posting an Instagram photo of it, that's going to be very, very hard for you to watch. It's going to feel like a personal attack on your spiritual practice.

People really seem to get offended only when something is true. When people say things about me on the internet that are untrue, it's easy to brush it off. But when someone posts something that hits home, especially if it's something I didn't want to own up to, that stings. The troubling irony is that the same thing that makes comedy work is the very thing that is most likely to upset people: TRUTH.

THE NOT-SO-MAGIC KINGDOM

All my biggest videos exist at that sweet spot where funny meets true. They're pointing out everyday hypocrisy. One of my most successful viral videos of all time is called "Every Parent at Disney." It has more than twenty-five million views and was shared by, among others, the *Today Show,* CNN, and practically every morning show and mom blog in America. Basically, the video portrays what parents *really* deal with when they spend a day at the Magic Kingdom.

The idea was birthed after I saw a Disney World commercial on TV. Kids were smiling, skipping around the park, licking ice cream cones while wearing mouse ears, hugging their parents, and telling them how much they loved them. I've been to Disney both as a child and as an adult. I don't have kids, but I know for a fact that it doesn't go down like that.

The reality is, kids get tired. It's incredibly hot. The lines are long. The Elsa doll in the gift shop doesn't come in the right color. The fourteen-dollar ice cream cone melts and runs down the little girl's arm while Mom, burdened down with diaper bags and lightsabers, frantically scrounges for a napkin, and Dad checks ESPN. That's reality. That's the truth that the video tapped into. And that spreads. The comments on the video were so telling:

- "How you managed to capture my husband's EXACT Disney behavior is beyond me."
- "I work at the Magic Kingdom and this couldn't be any more accurate."
- "Finally, a 'real' advertisement for Disney."
- "This gave me flashbacks to our Disney World trips. I'm pretty sure Mom used some of these exact phrases."

Usually, those comments tagged the siblings, parents, and friends they'd traveled with to Disney. People they knew could relate. It's funny because everyone seems to agree that this is the truth, yet all the photos we post of our trips to Disney look more like the unrealistic commercial. I hate to say it, but we're just lying. We're lying to ourselves, and we're lying to our followers. Sure, smiling as a family in front of the Magic Kingdom *did* happen, but a lot of other things also happened: The line for Space Mountain took three hours. The kids got scared and started crying when they met Captain Hook. Mom caught Dad staring at a woman in a tank top and was passive-aggressive with him all afternoon. The distance between the truth and reality is where the funny always lies.

CAN'T WIN 'EM ALL

A few years ago, I was living in Los Angeles. Christians in L.A. are different than in the rest of the country. Different how, you say? Like, there was a red carpet and a photo wall outside the church. Paparazzi photographers were always trying to catch whichever celebrity was attending that week.

But seeing people like Justin Bieber in church was just one of the ways that popular churches in L.A. were different from the ones in Middle America. In L.A., the pre-service playlist was hip-hop. All the pastors looked like runway models. For a while, I became immersed in that lifestyle. Spending a lot of time in church out there, that's what I ingested. If you grew up where I did—where pastors wore pleated khakis and button-ups, and the Bible came in the form of an actual book, not an iPad—this L.A. church scene could be pretty eye-opening.

So, I got the idea to do a video called "Swag Seminary." It was kind of a take on reality makeover shows, where two trendy dudes try to help a traditional pastor from Oklahoma connect with his congregation by making him look cooler. They give him new clothes and an updated haircut and recommend a sermon series called "Screenshotted: If Jesus had a Snapchat." It was pretty funny, but what I missed was that most people in the rest of America didn't have that experience of hipster pastors and trendy churches. It just wasn't relatable. The video fell flat.

Videos fail to connect with people for all sorts of reasons. I made a video once about how we all need to stop buying those books written by kids who claim to have died, gone to heaven, and come back. That was *not* a popular video. *At all*. I stand by the sentiment, though. Look, there are plenty of people thinking deeply and thoughtfully about life and death, heaven and hell—people who have studied religious and philosophy texts for years, debated deep questions with other smart people—but we're supposed to listen to what little Joey has to say on the subject? The theology of Charles Spurgeon? Nah. The insights of John Wesley? Not interested. No, impart to me Joey's great wisdom. This is a kid who you wouldn't believe if he told you that he lost his juice box, but now you're going to put your faith, your eternity, your entire understanding of the afterlife in a six-year-old's hands? It all seems kind of funny to me. I mean, really, if you're going to die and come back, can't you bring anything more useful with you than stories of Jesus on a rainbow-colored horse or about how you got to meet your great-granddad? Come on, Joey, how about some winning lottery numbers? A cure for cancer? Nothing?

The internet crushed me for that video. People felt I was taking a shot at sweet little kids who'd nearly died, but I really wasn't; I was taking a shot at those who were imbuing these sweet little kids' fantastical tales of the afterlife with the gravity of biblical truth. One of these kids who supposedly went to heaven and came back later retracted his story and admitted he told it only to get attention. Because . . . of course he did. He was *six*. Cut him some slack. At the time he made the story up, he'd never even read the Bible. It was only when he read it later, as a teenager, that he came clean. "People have profited from lies, and continue to," he said, referring to these kinds of books, including his own. "They should read the Bible, which is enough." Now, *that* Joey I can hang out with.

The essence of comedy is to pull ideas from people's collective subconscious, calling out truths that people haven't called out before. Jerry Seinfeld is the king of that. The way he starts so many of his jokes with, "Have you ever noticed . . ." has become such a trope that people sometimes make fun of him for it, but what he's doing is establishing a connection with his audience. Finding that common truth. I remember him doing a bit about seeing a hair stuck to the top tile in his shower and wondering how it got there, wondering what that hair's journey to the top tile looked like. It's silly, but it completely resonated with me to the point where I think about it every time I see a hair in the shower now.

I made a video a couple of years ago called "If Football Coaches Were Honest," which was another big one for me. The concept almost seemed too obvious. Every time I watch a football game, the postgame coach interview is always the same: "We tried our best." "We left it all on the field." "We've got a great group of kids in this locker room, and we'll correct our mistakes in practice this week." I decided to dress up as a football coach, go to an actual football game, and when the game ended go on the field and do the postgame interview, except using phrases that an *honest* football coach would say. My buddy Heath came with me to film it. I'll never forget standing down there on that grass, waiting for the game to end, and then sneaking onto the field to shoot the video, hoping I wouldn't get arrested. Then I spouted my nuggets of coaching honesty, about how the team didn't have enough good players, how the offensive coordinator was terrible, and how we were *definitely* going to lose again next week.

It went *huge*. ESPN, Bleacher Report, Barstool Sports, *Sports Illustrated*—they all picked it up. Nearly every comment underneath the video said some version of the same thing: "I wish a coach would actually talk like that."

More recently, I've been rolling out a series of videos called "Country Music Lyrics in Real Life." I love country music, but the videos poke fun at the distance between the fantasy world of country songs and the real world. If "Dirt Road Anthem" is your road map for living, you are for sure going to jail for a DUI in the near future. If your best ideas about romance were formed listening to Kenny Chesney's "She Thinks My Tractor's Sexy" or Brad Paisley's "Ticks," I feel bad for your girlfriend.

One of my biggest videos of the past couple of years is "Weatherman Melts Down on Live TV." It's just me, dressed as a weather reporter, standing in the snow, "reporting" on the snow falling all around me, getting increasingly salty with the news anchors back in the studio. The gist of it is pointing out how absurd it is that the local news station sends someone out to stand in bad weather, as if anyone watching the news couldn't just look out their window and see the weather for themselves. Yet it remains standard practice for any local news broadcast to subject their weatherman (or woman)—who probably has a graduate degree in meteorology—to snow, rain, sleet, hail, and hurricanes because somebody somewhere once decided those visuals pop on live television.

I can usually tell within the first fifteen minutes of uploading a video (often closer to the first five or ten minutes) whether it's going to be a hit. There's no magic to this. It's just a matter of paying attention. It's not about how many views a video is getting; it's how many times it's being shared. This is something that I learned when I was making videos for BuzzFeed back around 2015. They didn't care at all about views, only shares. If something is being shared a ton in those first fifteen minutes, you've got a good one on your hands. And almost always, it's being shared because people relate to something at the core of it.

I read a quote once that I loved so much that I entered it in my phone. I just scrolled back to find it: "If you want to tell people the truth, make them laugh. Otherwise they'll kill you." The internet says that Oscar Wilde first coined that phrase, although I'm pretty sure I read it in an interview with Richard Pryor. Regardless, that's real talk right there. Humor has the ability to disarm people, and once you've disarmed them, the truth can always sneak in the back door.

9

FOURSCORE AND SEVERAL YEARS AGO

My great-grandparents were Amish. My grandparents were Mennonite. My parents met at a Mennonite college. And then they had me. That should explain a lot.

Okay, well, let me see if I can elaborate a bit. You know Amish people, right? It's a *very* traditional lifestyle. They live on farms in Pennsylvania and those types of places? Ride horse-and-buggies and have bowl cuts? They don't believe in electricity, and all the women wear head coverings? Yeah, that was my great-grandparents, more or less. They didn't believe in war or technology or modern healthcare. They didn't go to the doctor, because they believed God can heal the body. Kind of like those snake-handling Pentecostal churches, but with a lot fewer snakes. (Okay, actually no snakes.)

My grandparents kind of broke away from the Amish lifestyle (they had electricity!) but still largely maintained the same religious beliefs. They were Mennonites. That's like Amish but with a TV. I'm sure some Mennonites are gonna read this and disagree with that description—and, okay, yes, sure, that's maybe an oversimplification—but that's the easiest way I know how to describe it.

My grandfather was a conscientious objector during Vietnam and maintained a long-running aversion to technology and the modern world. When we'd visit for Thanksgiving, no one was allowed to have phones or screens. No microwaves either. I remember my mom having to cook a hot dog in boiling water when we were over there. I get that was intended as a noble stand against the modern world, but what about all the technology that went into processing that meat into a hot dog? Is there an Old Testament verse that explains that?

My parents were strict. There were lots of rules. No long hair. No hats at the dinner table. Sit up straight. Tuck in your shirt. You get the picture. Obviously, alcohol was forbidden in our house. I picked up an empty beer bottle on our street once, and we came pretty close to performing an exorcism that night.

My parents have gone to great lengths in their own lives to enforce this prohibition against alcohol. I was told they went to a dinner party a few years ago and when they found out the pasta sauce being served was cooked with white wine, they didn't eat. The fact that the alcohol actually burns off when you cook didn't matter. They sat there in silent protest, not eating. My mom claims that story isn't true, but that's how my friend Christie remembers it! Either way, it's a pretty funny—and pretty spot-on—description of my parents. I love them for it. I respect the moral commitment. Honestly, I *wish* I had that kind of restraint. My last New Year's resolution was to quit caffeine. I made it six days.

My dad grew up on a farm in Lancaster County, in southern

Pennsylvania, among the Amish. He was up every morning at 4 A.M. to do the milk run and start his chores. I don't know much about the milk business in those days, but I do know you had to be dependable—never late, no sick days. Rain, sleet, or snow, the milk needed to be on the doorstep. That meant efficiency was important in his house. So was living up to your responsibilities. If you're supposed to be at work, you show up. That was drilled into my dad, and he drilled it into his own kids.

My mom's family was even more Mennonite than my dad's. It's a huge family. She was one of five kids and then had eight kids herself, but most of her siblings have even more kids than she does. Everyone in the clan was homeschooled. Her father would often take us to Billy Graham crusades and that sort of thing.

But appearances could be deceiving, particularly in my dad's family. In many ways, they were just like how we all are now: trying to appear to be better, more righteous people than they really were. When you scratched the surface of their godly exterior, things got really weird really quickly. My grandmother was what might politely be called "a character."

She and my grandfather owned a dairy farm. It was very successful, and it made them rich, a fact that my grandmother clearly enjoyed flaunting. Her hair was always permed eight inches high, and she liked to wear mink coats, along with lots of jewelry and gold. She basically looked like a rapper, but an old white lady. She used to tell us all these elaborate stories about meeting John F. Kennedy or other famous people. I only later found out that these tales were a *bit* exaggerated. We'd go to her house for Christmas and I'd see George Bush's family Christmas card displayed proudly on her mantel. I'd think, *My grandma is friends with the president?* Come to find out, everyone who donated to his campaign got a Christmas card. She didn't know him at all.

When I was growing up, my grandma presided over the extended family as its towering matriarch. We were all constantly having to perform for her in ways that seem a little odd when I think about them now. Around the holidays, we would play this game called Pass the Cash, where my grandma would stand at the top of the stairs with a handful of one-dollar bills and make it rain down on me and all my siblings and cousins. *For real.* We would scramble down below her grabbing at the money. This serves as a pretty good metaphor for her relationship with most of her children and grandchildren. She had money and used it as leverage to exert authority and command affection. There were constant jokes about how she was going to take you out of her will if you did something to upset her. But they kind of weren't jokes.

When I was young, whenever we'd go up to Pennsylvania to see my grandparents, we'd interact a bit with Amish culture. I'd see the Amish neighbors riding in their horse-and-buggies or all dressed the same while working in the fields. It didn't look like much fun. I was like, *Wait, so they clearly know about cars, and their lives would clearly be a lot easier if they had one. I don't know how many miles per hay bale a horse gets, but it can't be as efficient as a car. And man, if they had a tractor instead of having to pull their plows behind a horse, they could plow so much faster!*

But my thoughts on that lifestyle have changed as I've gotten older. The last time we went back there for Christmas, my sister-in-law said something like, "They must see me wearing makeup and having a cellphone and be very jealous." And I was like, "You know what? I don't think they are."

Think about it: They've all chosen this lifestyle. I mean, are we any happier than they are? I doubt it. I've got a cellphone *and* also a prescription for antidepressants. So, who's the real winner here? Shoot, sometimes that simpler way of life attracts me. I mean, I probably wouldn't be of much use on a farm—my hands have too much moisturizer on them—but I *am* good at shuffleboard.

It's been interesting to see, as I and all my siblings became adults, which parts of our ancestors' traditional values we adopted and which ones we didn't. Some of my siblings don't drink, and some do. I don't think any of us have tattoos—another cardinal sin among the Amish—but I think my little sister knits for fun, which seems like a very Amish-approved activity.

OVER THE RIVER AND THROUGH THE WOODS

Every Christmas, my whole family would go up to my grandparents' house in Pennsylvania. One of the Christmas traditions was to put on a talent show. I might play a song on the piano or spell some words from that year's vocabulary textbook (real basic stuff), my cousin Jesse would do a magic trick, and another cousin would tap-dance or play the trumpet. Everyone had to do their little bit before they'd get their Christmas present.

This tit-for-tat arrangement made my grandma's Christmas gifts—and, by extension, her love and approval—seem like something we had to work for. It was conditional. And this wasn't just when we were little kids. It continued well into adulthood. After I'd started doing comedy, those next couple of Christmases, I was expected to do a set for my grandmother. Which was absurd. She didn't get any of my jokes. I was doing stuff about texting and driving, online dating, and Snapchat filters—she had no idea what on earth I was talking about.

One of the first really solid bits I had was about these Cash-4Gold commercials I'd seen on television. "So you're telling me there's this envelope being filled up with gold and then you address it to 'Cash4Gold' and put it in your mailbox? That's a good plan until the mailman comes and picks up this Cash-4Gold envelope that weighs ten pounds. He's for sure quitting that day. How about that lucky postman who has the Cash-4Gold warehouse on his route? Anything coming in or out of that building is either cash or gold!" The bit worked in the clubs, and when I did it at Christmas, all my cousins loved it. But my grandma? She didn't even have a TV. But that wasn't the point. She wanted us to perform for her.

One year I decided I was over it. I mean, I'd played some terrible gigs before, but this was kind of the worst. In comedy, the setting really matters, as does the audience, and standing in front of the fireplace at my grandparents' farm, with my grandmother looking on, was far from the right vibe. In comedy parlance, it was not a warm room. Besides, by this point, I was old enough to realize there was something very wrong with adult children being made to perform for their grandmother. So I went on strike. A month or two before Christmas, I made it clear I wasn't doing a comedy show that year, nor was I going to perform any kind of talent. It turned into a big deal. After all, we had been doing these talent shows since we were little, and here I was, someone who did their "talent" for a living, refusing to be a dancing monkey.

I'm not sure if my refusal was more personal or professional. I mean, sure, I was standing up to my grandmother, but part of it was I just didn't want to do a show that wouldn't be at all reflective of the kind of performances I was capable of. I'd crush at the comedy club, but there's no way I'd be able to do that following my niece singing "Silent Night." And I felt like my profession was kind of being judged based on how good (or bad) my performance was, so I said I wasn't doing it anymore.

The night of the talent show, my dad pulled me aside and looked at me very seriously.

"John, you have to do the comedy show."

I shook my head. "I'm not going to."

"Your grandmother is going to be really disappointed."

I thought about this. My grandmother didn't care. She was old. I could've been reading the Gettysburg Address, for all she knew. The only one who really cared was him. He was afraid to disappoint her, not to perform—that he would get disinherited or whatever she might threaten to do. Personally, I didn't care about her money anymore. I mean, at this point in my comedy career, I was definitely still working for comped bar tabs and free appetizers and didn't have any money, so I'm not sure where I summoned the moral conviction from.

I didn't do the show. It was a real coming-of-age type of moment. I wish it would've happened when I was eighteen or so, but I was actually in my late twenties by this time. Nevertheless, that day I started to understand something important about the relationships between children and their parents: They may be formed when we're young, but they don't stop when we turn eighteen or move out of the house.

Funny thing is, all this seeking-the-approval-of-your-parents stuff—I still do it, so I can't exactly fault my dad for it. I remember when I got bumped up to what was called the "Almost Famous" list at the Comedy Works in Denver. That was basically the highest achievement at the club. It meant that I could work weekends, opening for people like Joe Rogan and Dave Chappelle. It was a huge honor and a big deal. The first people I called were my parents. But they didn't get it. At all.

"Does that mean you get paid more?"

"No, but I get to work on the weekends now."

"And that's a good thing?"

Sigh. The first time I ever did comedy on television, it was the same. I flew to New York to do stand-up at the Gotham Comedy Club for a TV show called *Live at Gotham.* I posted something about the rehearsal on Instagram, and the internet went nuts: thousands of likes, hundreds of comments, DMs from other comics congratulating me. I had arrived. I had made it. I called my parents and told them the news. This was 2014 and my dad had actually become the mayor of my hometown and, by then, my parents finally owned a TV. I expected that they would invite all the neighbors over or maybe even put up a projector at city hall for a watch party. But all they said was, "Oh, we don't get that channel." It was like I was back on that curb at the tennis center waiting for someone to pick me up, all over again. It was a replay of an old script telling me that I was unseen and unloved. The pain was real.

I'll never forget what happened next, which only further ingrained all the old scripts. That first television appearance went amazingly. Louie Anderson, the legendary stand-up comic, was the host. There were lights and cameras and cues and all this stuff I'd never dealt with before, but I did well with all of it. I felt proud. I walked out of that club having nailed my first television appearance and back onto the dark streets of New York. It didn't matter that I'd just killed in front of millions on TV—now I was back to being a nobody. Back to not being able to hail a cab (should've used Uber I guess). Back to waiting in line to purchase a ticket for the subway, staring at the map and not even knowing which direction I needed to go to get to my hotel.

A female comedian I'd met back in Denver a year or so earlier who lived in New York had come to the taping. She texted to ask if I wanted to meet up with her. The choice at that point was pretty simple: Go back to my hotel room and cope with the comedown of being on television all alone, or meet up with her and keep the high going. Of course you know what I chose.

We got some Bud Light and went back to the hotel room together. This is the part of the story I'll never forget. We were lying on the bed talking—about the TV appearance, about comedy, about whatever—and then she suggested we engage in some very adult activities together, which at that point in my life I'd never done.

"Uh, what do you mean?" I stammered.

"You were on TV tonight," she said. "You deserve it."

We never ended up doing much besides kissing, but what stuck with me, what cemented that moment in my brain so deeply, what makes me recall that moment like it happened yesterday, was that statement of hers: "You were on TV tonight. You deserve it."

I had just had the biggest moment of my professional career, maybe the biggest moment of my life, and my parents, from whom I desperately wanted approval, had not seen it. But lo and behold, this woman offered me all the attention I could've ever wanted. Consciously or subconsciously, I made a mental note of it.

10

WELCOME TO MY TED TALK

In ninth grade, I stood a towering four feet eleven inches tall and weighed about eighty-five pounds. I looked like that kid from *Rugrats,* except I was in high school. I'd grown up playing basketball on the courts in the park across the street from my house and in a homeschool basketball league that I remember mostly because, as I mentioned before, they made us wear long pants. I loved basketball and thought I was pretty good at it. I wasn't, but at that age, perception is reality. Or it was for me. So when the ninth grade began at Providence, I decided to try out for the basketball team.

Coming from homeschool, this felt like a grown man's world. But in terms of schools, it was still just single A. In Georgia, that means the smallest-possible school. My graduating class had about ninety people in it. Nonetheless, for three days, I turned up to the gym and ran through various drills and scrimmages. I thought I played okay, but you might be surprised to find out that in high school basketball, even at a tiny Christian private school, there is not a tremendous demand for wispy four-feet-eleven-inch kids with limited athletic ability. I can still remember after that third day of tryouts, Coach Mac went into his office and closed the door while all of us hopefuls just milled around outside nervously. Then the door opened, and he posted the list on the wall, then went back in his office. All the kids, including me, ran to read the list.

My eyes scanned for . . .

John Crist . . .

John Crist . . .

John Crist . . .

It wasn't on there.

I read through it again, confused. Yep, no *John Crist* up there.

It was the first time I'd ever been cut from anything. Rejection stings. It really does. Especially when it's public. It's embarrassing. When I think back to that moment, amid a scrum of my friends, reading over that list once, then twice, to make sure I hadn't missed my own name, I can still feel that pang of disappointment. Your stomach drops. The blood drains from your face a little. You wish you could curl up in a ball and disappear. It doesn't get better that night when you go home. How will you face your friends at school the next day? They all know you wanted to play. They all know that you failed.

This is another frozen moment in time for me. I remember it all so well: the white cinder-block wall, the woodgrain office door, the red-and-blue basketball court, the carpet, and the message reverberating through it all: *Go home. We don't want you here. We want these other kids, not you. You are not worthy. You are not loved.*

I sort of can't believe they still do this at schools. In some ways, I think it's too much for kids to handle. I remember the cheerleaders had tryouts, and they all got envelopes and headed to their cars to open them alone with their parents. I suppose that's a little less embarrassing. But for me, that day was brutal. I imagine that now it's even worse: Someone takes a photo of that list, posts it to Instagram, and tags everyone in your grade at school. What was once your semiprivate failure becomes a public spectacle. Soon it's not just the kids at school who know you're not even good enough to ride the pine at one of the smallest high schools in the state; all your relatives know too, as do your friends from church, your pastor, your neighbors, and that girl you met last summer at camp who you bragged to about being really good at basketball. I'm sure it feels like the modern version of getting rotten vegetables pelted at you in the town square. No wonder everyone has all this anxiety and stress.

Embarrassment sometimes feels more public than it really is, though. During my senior year at Providence, I had a huge crush on a girl named Lacey. Prom was around the corner, and my mind was made up: Me and Lacey were gonna go together. I'd give her one of those flower things you put around your wrist, and then we'd slow dance to "Strawberry Wine." (Hey, it was a Christian school, so "Back That Thang Up" was not allowed.) Anyway, after a basketball game one Friday night, we were all hanging out at her house. She walked over to the kitchen to get a drink, and I saw an opening. I casually walked over to the kitchen as well and somehow mustered up the courage to say, "Hey, Lacey, do you want to go to prom with me?"

Hard no.

The exact same feeling as not seeing my name on the basketball roster.

In fact, she told me that she was hoping our buddy Josh would ask her but he hadn't yet. I was devastated. The rejection stung badly, but my belief that everyone knew that I'd been rejected made it a hundred times worse. My first thought was, *There is no way I can go to school tomorrow. Everyone will be looking at me as I walk down the halls, snickering and making comments about how Lacey said no to me, about what a loser I was.* I was seriously wondering whether it was possible for me to transfer to another school.

We spend all our lives so focused on our own lives that we eventually start thinking that everyone else is thinking about us too. But they're not. They're thinking about themselves. It would have been nice if I could have learned that lesson back then, but all these years later, I still kind of think that. *My video this week didn't get as many views as normal. I bet everyone is talking about how much of a failure I am.* The truth is, we each may be the biggest star of the movie playing in our own head, but in everyone else's head, we're just extras.

I GOT NEXT

For me, back then, getting cut from the basketball team or being turned down for prom felt like the end of the world. It wasn't, of course. In fact, I've come to believe that the way we learn to handle our rejections and failures is about as important as anything we learn in our lives. No one's life is an endless series of triumphs. (Or if anyone's is, we are all completely justified in hating that person.) In most people's lives, disappointment is far more common than success. If every one of those disappointments puts you in the fetal position, if it keeps you from trying again to achieve the things you want, if it causes you to lose sight of those things entirely, life is probably going to be miserable.

I read that in Joel Osteen's book. Just kidding. But I know that sounds kind of self-helpish. I'm sure there's a poster on the ceiling of your dentist's office with a cute kitten on it and a slogan that will tell you this exact same thing. But sometimes sayings become clichés because they're true. Learning to bounce back from failure might be the most important skill you can learn as a kid. If I didn't learn it as a kid, I certainly have as an adult! Sadly, we seem intent on slowly erasing it from life, or at least trying to.

I go to see my friends' kids play soccer now and find out they're not allowed to keep score anymore. At the end of the season, everyone gets a trophy. Sports are inherently competitive. Learning how to win and lose with grace is kind of the point. Discovering what you're good at, what you're not good at, and how to best contribute to a team regardless is all part of the journey. We're not all equally good at everything. That's not the way the world works. So why are we trying to teach kids this? No wonder they get out into the world and fall apart at the first sign of adversity.

In the case of me and the Providence Christian Academy basketball team, I will have you know that I simply dusted myself off, worked harder, went back to the next season's tryouts, and became the team's star point guard. Just kidding. That's Michael Jordan's story. I for sure quit. I never tried out for the basketball team again. I looked around and realized there were many people who were clearly much better than me at basketball and that my life would be perfectly fine if I didn't play for the Providence team.

Without basketball practices to go to that winter, I focused my attention on tennis, which I found suited my personality much better anyway. It's a game for a single man, 'cause ya know I can't have all these teammates out there holding me back! Okay, that's maybe not exactly it, but I got really good at tennis. And for real, I liked playing alone. I didn't have to worry about anyone else missing a shot or disappointing all my teammates by making a bad pass. I loved that it was all on me. I'm sure the fact that I ended up in a profession that is definitely a solo gig is not a coincidence.

Getting cut from the basketball team and being turned down for prom were important lessons for me to learn. Rejection became a daily part of my existence once I started to do comedy. *No, we don't think you're funny. No, we can't put you on the show on Friday night. No, you're not the right look for this audition. No, your comedy isn't funny enough for late-night.* I guess that over time, you build up a thick skin. Rejection hurts less. Or maybe it doesn't hurt any less, but the knowledge that it is not terminal, but temporary, certainly makes it easier to deal with. Persistence and ingenuity will eventually wear rejection down. Ambition will run it off the road. Maybe all that rejection helped me not to be scared of it, at least professionally.

Back when I was just starting out as a stand-up, when most of what I was hearing from people was no, I took a comedy-boot-camp class at a club in Denver that was taught by Louie Anderson and a comic named Kyle Cease. It cost about three hundred dollars, which was a lot of money for me at the time, but Louie was a world-famous comic—this was years before he hosted my first TV appearance—and I saw this class as a chance to learn from him. There were about a hundred of us in there, and he offered us tips on booking shows, getting an agent, and working on material. At the end of the class, he told everyone, "If any of you are ever in Vegas, hit me up. I do a regular show out there at the Excalibur."

There were hundreds of comics in the room that day, so of course he couldn't really accommodate that offer. Maybe he was just saying it to be nice. But I wasn't afraid to hear the word *no*. So the next week, I booked a flight to Las Vegas. I emailed Louie, telling him I was ready to take him up on his offer and that I'd be there Friday night. I fully expected to get rejected. But he responded right away: "Sounds good. Do you want to do ten minutes on the show?"

I couldn't believe it. At the time, I was a glorified open micer. This was a gig opening for a famous comic on the Las Vegas Strip. This was a huge break. I did not let the fact that I knew that I didn't have ten good minutes of material stop me from saying yes.

I will never forget that day. Walking through the airport, I felt like a star. *If only all these people knew how famous I was,* I thought. I got there and took a cab to Harrah's because I couldn't afford to stay at the Excalibur. I wrote myself a little cheat sheet to help me remember my jokes, ironed my shirt, and headed to the Excalibur. About an hour before the show, I walked up to the box office and told the guy I was on the show. He escorted me back to the greenroom.

When I think back to that night, I can still feel the rush. The host asked me for my name and where I was from, as if he were about to introduce an actual professional comedian. I stood at the bottom of the backstage stairs, wearing jeans and a forest-green button-up shirt, while the host went up onstage and did his set. Then he said, "Before we bring out Louie, we have a very special guest with us tonight. Please welcome all the way from Denver, Colorado, John Crist!" I walked out there. The lights were very bright, and the crowd was loud. I grabbed the microphone—it was cordless, and I'd never done a show with a cordless mic before—and did my ten minutes.

And I did well. I didn't get a standing ovation or anything, but I held my own. I felt like I belonged there. It was surreal. After the show, I was walking out and someone asked me for my autograph. She asked *me* if I could sign her ticket stub. It was the first autograph I ever gave. I tried to act really casual about it, like "Yeah, yeah, no problem" as if it were some sort of inconvenience for me. But I would've paid her to ask me. It felt incredible, and that feeling coursed through my veins as I walked back to Harrah's. Or I may have levitated—not sure.

11

MY PLEASURE

If you've followed me for any amount of time online, you probably know that I like Chick-fil-A. One of the first jokes I ever wrote was about Chick-fil-A: "I just moved to a new city and I haven't found a church to go to yet. So in the meantime, I've been giving my tithe money to this Christian organization that feeds the hungry . . . Chick-fil-A." (I don't care what you say—that's an A-plus joke.) The fast-food chain is ripe for jokes, and I've got lots of them. I've made videos titled "Chick-fil-A Pickup Lines," "Chick-fil-A HR Department," and "Chick-fil-A Drug Dealer." I probably eat there three times a week, so if the old comedy adage is to write what you know, Chick-fil-A is what I know.

If I try to uncover why I like Chick-fil-A so much, I'm drawn back to the fact that there was one right down the street from my house when I was growing up. It opened when I was about ten years old, and after that, it always felt like a delicacy in our family. In terms of fast food, it was sort of expensive, at least for a kid without a steady source of income. When I went to private school, we'd have to pack our own lunches, but on Fridays, they'd cater Chick-fil-A. All the kids around me would buy one chicken sandwich, if not two. But they were $2.50, and I could never afford one. I was stuck eating a sad-looking PB&J that I'd made for myself that morning. It's a feeling I'll never forget. Maybe that's why I love Chick-fil-A so much now. I can afford it. Started from the bottom, and now we here!

The first job I ever had was working at a Chick-fil-A. It was the one within walking distance of my house. There was a Burger King in the same area, but my mom wouldn't let me dare associate with those heathens. I was fifteen then and had only recently started attending a private Christian school, after being homeschooled through seventh grade, so this job was part of a period in my life when I was like an animal raised in captivity, then slowly being released into the wild. You know how some animals have a litter of babies, expecting that some won't make it to adulthood? This was my house growing up. Jumping off the roof while using an umbrella as a parachute? Using the trampoline to launch my little brother over the fence into the neighbor's pool? These were the things that happened at The Crist House. Anyway, fifteen was right about the age that my parents were like, "You know our third kid, John? Yeah, he might just make it!"

That Chick-fil-A job was also about the time in my life when *I* knew I was going to make it too. I walked in and there was an immediate sense from my first day that I belonged. These were my people. The owner liked me. All the other kids on my shifts thought I was funny. The Latino cooks nicknamed me "Colocho," which I was told means "Q-tip" in Spanish, and which I have avoided looking up for fear it might have been a far less endearing nickname.

I worked at the register, I worked the drive-through, and, despite how much I loved the job—and I can say this with all the wisdom I've gained in the twenty-plus years since then—I was an absolutely terrible employee. Awful. I didn't know how to do anything, and I didn't care that I didn't know how to do anything. I would bread the chicken, accidentally drop it on the floor, and then just toss it into the fryer without a second thought. For sure, this was not in line with company policy, but, to me, my actions had their own internal logic: It was a thousand degrees in that fryer. Whatever germs the chicken may have collected on the floor of the kitchen would surely be seared off in that cauldron. Plus, this is the Lord's chicken anyway—it's pre-blessed. Have you ever heard of anyone getting sick from eating Chick-fil-A? That's what I thought. One time a customer complained that there was a hair in his salad, so I took off the tomato that had the hair on it, replaced it with a tomato from one of the sandwiches, and gave him back the same salad. He was livid. I thought it was pretty funny.

Full confession: I also stole some food while I worked there. (I am fairly certain the statute of limitations for Chick-fil-A theft has run out, so I'm in the clear legally.) My buddies and I had a system all worked out. They'd come in when I was working, I'd see them, and I'd automatically grab a tray. I'd fill it with food, then hand it to them as if they'd just ordered and paid for it: "Let's see, five chicken sandwiches, two nuggets, three fries, and four drinks. Here you go, sir." It could not have been more obvious. I still kind of feel bad about this. Actually, my high school buddies should feel bad. They are the ones who consumed the stolen food, not me!

I kept screwing stuff up when I worked there. Three months

in, I already had a few priors on my record. I remember them often sending me out into the parking lot with a broom and dustpan. I literally swept the parking lot, mostly picking up cigarette butts. I remember one hot Saturday afternoon, the place was packed and everybody wanted lemonade. We ran out of it, and the manager said, "CRIST! Go in back and make some more lemonade NOW!" I ran to the back and got the big five-gallon bucket to mix everything in.

I could hear my fellow employees at the registers entreating me to hurry up. "John, how's the lemonade coming?" "I need five lemonades!" I poured the lemon juice in, added sugar, then poured in water. "John, lemonade!" "Is it ready yet?" I scrambled to find the big industrial spoon thing that I was supposed to mix the lemonade with, but it was nowhere to be found. "JOHN, WHERE IS THAT LEMONADE?" "WE NEED LEMONADE NOW!" Starting to panic, and still unable to find the spoon, I improvised, rolling up my sleeve past my elbow and sticking my whole arm into the jug to stir the mixture. Just then, my manager came to the back to check on my progress and found me nearly shoulder deep in the lemonade. He looked at me, almost more befuddled than angry, like, *What kind of person would actually do that?* I thought it was pretty ingenious.

"Hey," he said, shaking his head. "I'm not sure Chick-fil-A is the place for you." He might as well have just told me I wasn't going to heaven either. I was never actually fired, but I suddenly started appearing on the schedule less and less. Pretty soon I wasn't on the schedule at all. I thought, *Maybe the place closed.* Nope. Sure enough, it's still open to this day. Come to think of it, the next time you're on the corner of Highway 29 and Indian Trail in Lilburn, Georgia, stop in, ask for the manager, and tell him that John Crist was wrongfully terminated. That would make my life.

Now that I'm apparently in the Chick-fil-A confessional, I got one more story. I feel like this one was pretty clever, although also a little sinister. In college at Samford, we had a Chick-fil-A in the student center. It was one of a bunch of restaurants there, part of a food court. You could get your tray, then grab food from Chick-fil-A, Subway, wherever, then go to the register and pay. The chicken biscuits cost about three bucks each, but just a plain buttered biscuit cost like fifty cents. My buddy Daniel concocted a plan. All the biscuits were wrapped specifically to say what was inside them. Daniel thought that if he rewrapped it to say "buttered," we could start getting chicken biscuits for fifty cents. And it worked! It seems kind of ironic that we did that for years, all the while paying about twenty grand annually to go to school there. But we were broke college kids whose parents covered tuition, not meals. So those savings/stealings mattered.

Years later, I was performing at a Chick-fil-A corporate event and I told that exact story, admitting to executives at the company that I stole a bunch of chicken biscuits and felt bad about it. They thought it was hilarious. They'd never thought of that loophole in their system and thanked me for alerting them to it. I guess I also owe an apology to all the hungry college students who now have to pay full price for those biscuits. My bad. #snitchesgetstitches.

As it is, I've made so many Chick-fil-A related Insta stories and tweets that I feel like I've repaid them in free advertising. Shoot, go to Chick-fil-A for lunch tomorrow (unless it's a Sunday) and tell them it's your first time there, that you only heard about the place after reading John Crist's book, and how he talked about it so fondly. That will surely clean my conscience.

THE ITALIAN SODA JOB

Chick-fil-A represents one pillar of my Holy Trinity of fast food. The other two pillars, Taco Bell and McDonald's, have equally emotional roots.

When I was growing up, we were not poor, but there wasn't much in the way of disposable income to go around. Dad was a pastor, Mom homeschooled us, and there were a lot of us—eight kids in all—so any expense was automatically multiplied by eight. New shoes, new clothes, Christmas presents—there were no small expenses. So going out to eat was just not something we did very often. It was a big deal. After church, when most families would go out to lunch together, we'd always go home to eat. My mom's cooking was amazing, but we didn't care. All we could think about was our friends living the high life at Golden Corral.

But every once in a long while, we'd get a treat. There was a Taco Bell right next to our church, and on those rare occasions when Dad would announce, "We're going to Taco Bell for lunch," all eight of us would act as if we'd just won the lottery. We'd go nuts. When we got there, there was no looking at the menu and choosing what we might want. That choice was made for us. We'd always get soft tacos, which cost about sixty cents each back in the nineties. Dad would order something like forty of them, stacked on a huge tray, and one large refillable fountain drink that we would pass around between us. We were kings for a day. If there had been social media in 1994 and my parents let ten-year-old John have an Instagram account, I'd have posted a photo of myself behind that tray of forty tacos with the caption "Can't hide money."

By the way, I never gave it much thought back then, but buying one drink and sharing it between ten of us maybe crosses an invisible line between sharing and stealing. I get a kick out of the fact that my father, a strictly religious evangelical pastor who otherwise lives by the Ten Commandments, could justify this to himself. I certainly don't hold it against him. I think all of us tell ourselves little stories to justify our humanity.

We each tend to draw our own lines in the sand when it comes to things like stealing. Is it stealing to ask for a free cup of water at Taco Bell and then fill it with Sprite? I'd say yes, but it's clearly not a capital crime. What about buying an expensive suit, wearing it once to take a headshot for one's tour poster, and then returning it? I've done that. Is sharing a Netflix password with a friend stealing? I think most people would probably say no, but they'd certainly consider swiping a DVD off the shelf at Walmart and running out of the store with it stealing. Isn't sharing a Netflix password kind of equivalent to stealing a huge truck full of DVDs? Essentially, you're Italian Jobbing the whole place. But we make these little deals with ourselves to convince ourselves that we're good people, that we're not *really* doing anything wrong.

I remember being at a FedEx/Kinko's once, laminating a few things, then looking at the line to pay and seeing that it snaked almost out the door. I owed them literally forty cents. I was in a rush and thought, *Forget it—I'll just pay them extra next time,* and walked out. There was no next time, though, because it then became impractical. How am I going to explain why I want to pay for three laminates that I'm not actually buying?

How are they going to ring them up? Ultimately, I decided FedEx was unlikely to go under because of my laminate thievery and just moved on with my life. (But if FedEx reads this and wants their forty cents back, I'm happy to make good on my debt. With interest.) At any rate, I've always had a real affection for Taco Bell for not calling my family out on our soda heist, which surely would've ruined those magical Sundays when my family was polishing off a pyramid of beef tacos. And I've eaten there ever since.

MCEMBASSY

My attachment to McDonald's is perhaps the most convoluted to explain. It began one summer during college in the unlikeliest of locales, a city in central Morocco called Fes. So how did I end up spending my summer in Morocco? Well, all those reading this who are thinking, *Oh fun! Morocco! I love the Caribbean!* you'll understand, because I thought the same thing when I signed up for this mission trip through my college.

Turns out, Morocco is in Africa. Who knew? (Homeschool geography only really covers the United States, because, well, of course it does.) Anyway, Morocco isn't even in the fun, *Lion King*–looking part of Africa. It's northern Africa, which was filled with dust, sand, and lots of people who looked, dressed, and talked much differently than me. Also, it was hot. Like really hot. Like however hot you're thinking right now, way hotter. Like 120-degrees-every-day hot. There was no air-conditioning, so every morning we'd wet a T-shirt and stick it in the freezer. At night, when we were ready to go to sleep, we'd put the frozen T-shirt on just to keep our body temperature down so we could sleep. *That* hot.

From the beginning, I could tell this was not going to be an easy three months. There were no cellphones, there was barely any internet, and I didn't speak a word of Arabic beyond "Salaam alaikum," which is kind of their version of "Whassup?" I remember flying into Casablanca and then taking a four-hour train ride across barren scrubland to Fes and thinking, *Lord, what have I gotten myself into?* We were told not to drink the water or buy local food like fruits, vegetables, or fish that might have been washed in the local water. This was also 2005, so a few years after 9/11, deep into the George W. Bush years, when Americans were not exactly everyone's favorite sons in North Africa and the Middle East. We were told that the country was hostile to Christians too, so I wasn't allowed to tell people I was doing a Christian mission. I was supposed to say I was visiting friends or on vacation. Also, because of religious sensitivities, we had to wear long sleeves and long pants wherever we went. Did I mention it was hot?

All these rules had me pretty freaked out upon arrival, and the first few weeks, I mostly just stayed in the apartment that the organizers had arranged for us. We were warned that the streets were filled with hustlers who would immediately zero in on us when we went out in public. They'd offer their services as guides, drivers, whatever. They'd try to sell us drugs. They'd want us to get in their taxis and charge us fifty dollars to go two miles, or they'd take us on tours of places where no one ever wanted to go. So we rarely went out, rarely talked to any locals. The only time I'd leave the apartment was with our local contact, a guy who would take me to the grocery store and to the site where I was supposed to be doing my missionary work. I was there ostensibly to make a documentary about an orphanage that had been funded by American evangelicals, but the truth is, I had no idea what I was doing. Just because I was a journalism major in college didn't mean I was qualified in any way whatsoever to make a compelling documentary.

The food in Morocco was okay, a lot of couscous and tagine, and every morning we could get fresh bread for the equivalent of about a nickel because it was subsidized by the government. But I was used to living off the food-court cafeteria at college, so it all felt really foreign. The simplest things felt impossible. I remember wanting to make change—you know, four quarters for a dollar, that kind of thing. How do you do that at a convenience store when you know exactly zero words in Arabic? Well, I hatched a plan and drew a bill and four coins on a piece of paper, then gave it to the cashier. It didn't work. He was even more confused. I think he thought I was trying to rob the place. It was those kinds of things, day after day. It was all so frustrating. But then, a glimmer of hope.

I started to hear rumors of a McDonald's somewhere in another part of the city. I immediately thought, *I would give literally anything to sink my teeth into a Big Mac.* But it seemed impossible. We were basically trapped in the apartment. I was told it just wasn't feasible to get there. But I was not going to be deterred. One Friday night, I got up the nerve, went out into the street, and hailed one of those supposedly predatory taxis. I asked to be taken to the part of town where I'd heard this McDonald's was located. Fortunately, the Arabic word for McDonald's is . . . wait for it . . . *McDonald's.* All I had to do was get in this taxi and say "McDonald's," and then, like magic, the cabdriver drove me to the only one in the city.

I remember the moment when that cab came around a hill

and I spotted the Golden Arches in the distance. I swear I heard an angel's choir and tipped my cap to the good Lord. It was just like that climactic scene in *Harold and Kumar Go to White Castle,* except that I hadn't smoked any weed.

Here's the crazy part: Not only did this McDonald's live up to my lofty expectations, but it blew those expectations out of the water. I can still feel the cool gust of glorious air-conditioning that hit me when I opened the front door. As I strode in, it was like I was engulfed in a cool cloud of wonderful refrigerated air. There were TVs inside playing American television. In fact, 50 Cent's "In da Club" was playing on MTV. And get this: I WAS HEARING OTHER PEOPLE SPEAK ENGLISH!

What was even crazier is that although in America McDonald's doesn't exactly attract the upper crust, in Morocco, McDonald's is strictly for ballers. The customers were rich. They were dressed up. This was the kind of crowd you might find at a classy rooftop bar in America. There were no pimply kids working the register; it was well-groomed middle-aged men. I was later told that working at McDonald's was considered one of the better jobs in the city because it was a rare place where you were guaranteed a paycheck. The economy could be volatile, corruption could be endemic, the government could be cutting its payrolls, but if you worked eight hours at McDonald's, you were getting paid for eight hours. I ordered in English, and everyone seemed happy to chat. It's difficult to describe just how comforting it was to have that human contact after living for weeks in what felt like near-total isolation.

I haven't even mentioned the best part yet: the food. It tasted *exactly the same* as it tastes in America. As soon as I took my first bite of my Big Mac, it was like immediately being transported back to Lilburn, Georgia. I decided at that moment that I would be spending the rest of my mission trip at this McDonald's. Suddenly Fes wasn't so scary and foreign. It was like McDonald's was the American Embassy, a little piece of home in a distant land.

Since that day, McDonald's has always comforted me. I'm sure I'm not the only one. I had a buddy, Nate, who shared the same affection. He was a colonel during the Iraq War, and there was one on his base in Iraq. It was a small reminder of home. Every week or so, he'd take a Friday lunch at McDonald's and wouldn't have wished to be at any other restaurant on earth.

That kind of comfort is something I have found myself drawn back to again and again. In a sense, fast food was my very first vice. Long before there was alcohol or women or any other bad habits to help ease the pain in my life, there were McDonald's, Taco Bell, and Chick-fil-A. (But only those three. I generally think fast food is gross and can't tell you the last time I ate at a Wendy's or a Burger King. Don't even get me started on Arby's.) When things have gotten rough for me, I have sometimes leaned on this fast-food triumvirate the way people lean on their friends and family. If you read that and worry that such behavior might not help someone become a solid, stable, emotionally healthy human being, well, you will undoubtedly be proven correct by the chapters that follow.

12

THAT GOOD MEDICINE

When I was growing up, we didn't have a TV in our house. My parents thought television was filled with sex, violence, and other worldly influences. To be fair, I suppose much of it was, so they believed they were protecting us by keeping us away from it. There were occasional exceptions. I distinctly remember my father bringing a television home—from church, of all places—so we could watch the Atlanta Braves in the 1995 World Series. Of course, because we had limited exposure to television, it felt all the more special when I did get to see it. It wasn't just a treat; it had an illicit quality that made it very appealing to a kid with a budding disdain toward anyone who was trying to tell him what he could or couldn't do.

This was the setting where I first began to discover stand-up comedy. I had to sneak it into my life, basically. My main partner in crime in my teenage years was my buddy Isaac. He was a real friend of the family, who I'd met in eighth grade when I started going to Providence. I'd sleep over at his house, and we'd sequester ourselves down in his basement, where we'd watch the BET weekly stand-up series *ComicView* while his parents were asleep upstairs. One night we snuck out of the house and went to see Martin Lawrence's stand-up film *Runteldat*. It blew my mind. Comedy, like so many other things in my life, started out as a secret.

When I went to college, my roommate freshman year, Louis, had one of those TV-and-DVD-player-combo things, and one of the DVDs he brought with him was the *Original Kings of Comedy,* the Spike Lee–directed stand-up film featuring Bernie Mac, Cedric the Entertainer, D. L. Hughley, and Steve Harvey. We'd watch that DVD practically every single day and walk around campus yelling out punch lines from it to each other. "Tell 'em I ain't got it!" was one of our favorite Cedric lines from that special, and me and Louis still quote it to each other to this day.

I'm not sure why I was particularly drawn to Black stand-up comedy back then, but it may have had something to do with the fact that it was often the rawest and most raucous comedy around. There was more to it than that, though. I loved the way audiences responded to those comics. They weren't just laughing. They were roaring. They were falling out of their chairs. They were dancing. They were shouting to the comics from the crowd. And Martin Lawrence or Bernie Mac or Cedric was up onstage soaking it all in and even conducting the crowd. The experience seemed almost spiritual. If you squinted just so, it looked a bit like church.

SIGN IT, STAMP IT, AND LICK IT

Back in 2007, my friend Lindsey invited me to a house party. I remember walking into a room there and finding two women who were sitting alone, staring raptly at a TV. I looked at what they were watching. There was a diminutive Black man, wearing a long white fur coat and matching white fedora, strutting onto the stage, flanked by a small harem of women, one of whom was carrying his large white goblet. It was the opening of a Katt Williams stand-up special, *The Pimp Chronicles*. I just stood there for two hours watching this special, jaw practically on the floor, in absolute amazement. Even though I had watched *Original Kings of Comedy* and *Runteldat,* this was another level altogether. To say he was killing doesn't even begin to describe what was happening in that auditorium. He absolutely owned that audience from the second he walked out there. He didn't even have to tell jokes to make the people explode. I'd never seen a performer wielding so much power. It was intoxicating.

By that time, I must have already begun thinking that stand-up was what I wanted to do with my life. My dad says that when I was a senior in high school and we went to visit some colleges, an admissions officer asked me what I wanted to do when I grew up and I told him, totally seriously, "I want to be Jay Leno." It never really occurred to me how unlikely this career plan was, particularly because I had no earthly idea how to go about achieving it. But I had seen Jay Leno on *The Tonight Show* and thought, *This is his job? Like, he does THIS for a living? I gotta figure out a way to do that.* I credit my parents, who had really drilled into me that anything was possible, and my own sheltered naivete, which had me thinking that being a comedian was as sensible a career option as becoming a lawyer or CPA. I didn't know any better.

Also, I guess there was something about being a pastor's kid that helped me believe I could make this dream happen. In a way, it's kind of like growing up in show business. I was always behind the scenes, in the greenroom, watching how my dad put on his show. Nothing about it seemed all that mysterious or unobtainable. I suppose I did realize as a skinny white Christian kid from Lilburn that I was not going to be Katt Williams. Jay Leno was a more realistic option.

The first comic I saw who really seemed like someone I could emulate was Brian Regan. I saw Regan's special *I Walked on the Moon* at Christmastime when I was about twenty. The craziest thing about seeing it was that I watched it with my parents and my ten-year-old sister. All Regan's jokes were pretty family friendly. I'd never heard of such a thing. He has a razor-sharp mind, and he is constantly pointing out the ridiculousness of modern life. He's universally respected in comedy circles and has become a stand-up star. His sense of humor jibed with my own, and his stand-up connected the two biggest loves of my life: my family and comedy. For years, I'd been sneaking off to watch comedy specials in my friends' basements, where my parents couldn't see me and disapprove, but suddenly I could enjoy comedy out in the open. It felt liberating.

WAIT, WHO *IS* THIS GUY?

I was always a funny kid. I loved to get up in front of the college group at my church and make them laugh, but I have a distinct memory of what I consider to be the first hard laugh I got as an adult. I was in college at the time, at Samford, a Christian college in Alabama. During a fraternity event, each of us had to introduce ourselves. "Hi, my name is Andrew Harrison, I'm from Pell City, and I'm a big Alabama football fan. Roll Tide!" "I'm Brian Cook. I'm from Knoxville, and I'm an engineering major." You get the idea.

Well, when it came around to my turn, I stood up, told
everyone my name, and then, completely straight faced, quoted
a line from a movie that is so foul-mouthed that I swore I'd
never repeat it. The actual joke itself is not really the point of
this story, though. It's about my learning the power of saying
something that no one expects you to say. There were about
250 people in the room, and the place exploded. People were
dying! I had never gotten a laugh like that, and I can still remember the feeling. That moment—the room, the lectern I
stood behind, the windows in the back of the room—is another
that is frozen in my mind. That feeling filled me up. For just a
moment, everything was okay. The attention I didn't get as a
child, the kids at Providence who bullied me, that emptiness of
limping home injured from basketball practice to a family too
busy to notice—it all melted away. All the broken pieces were
made whole. It was *that* powerful.

Church was my first real outlet to do comedy. After college,
I was living in Colorado Springs and would emcee events at
church or do stand-up bits for conferences here and there. I got
put in charge of making videos for the church announcements
each week and turned them into something of a training ground
for the viral videos that many people know me for now. The
videos were irreverent and often, frankly, pretty inappropriate,
but the pastor thought I was awesome and gave me pretty much
free rein. I remember being given the directive to announce the
new season of Bible studies—you know, the financial-peace
class was on Wednesdays, the Colossians Bible study was on Fridays, and so on. Anyway, I ended the announcement by advertising my own personal Bible study, exclusively for hot girls. It
was obviously a fake Bible study, but it was called "Marriage

And Konnected Emotions: Open, Unified, and Tender." I called it by its acronym: MAKEOUT. I honestly still think that was a pretty clever joke! Anyway, I got a stern lecture after that one, and the pastor definitely received some complaint emails.

I know it sounds immodest to say so, but my announcement videos became sort of a thing. People started showing up to services just because they'd heard about them. It was like having my own weekly show. I would sit in the back while the video played, and when it killed, when people were laughing, I'd get that same feeling I'd felt when I'd cracked up the meeting in my fraternity house: *All is good with my world. People like me.* I'd bathe in that feeling. When the video didn't do as well, I'd usually just go home. I didn't even stay for the rest of the church service. It was too embarrassing to face the crowd, so I didn't want to be in church anymore.

Church was a hugely important stage for me to start finding my way into comedy. Audiences there were on my side from the beginning, supporting me, rooting me on. I'd eventually even get my first road gig through church. Our pastor had a buddy who was the pastor of a church in Amarillo, and they invited me to do comedy for their youth conference, as I'd done for ours. So I drove to Amarillo and did an hour of comedy, and it went great. Then I got paid seven hundred dollars. At my nine-to-five job, it would have taken me two weeks of eight-hour shifts to make that much, so I thought I was rich.

But as important as church was as a launching pad for my comedy career, I also knew that if I wanted to really make it as a stand-up, I was going to have to venture from the cozy con-fines of church into the lions' den: an actual comedy club.

▓▓ JUNE 24, 2009

It took me a while to get up the nerve. I didn't really know any comedy clubs in Colorado, but during the summer of 2009, I was living back at home in Lilburn for a few months and decided to check out open-mic night at a club in Atlanta called the Laughing Skull Lounge. The first two times I went, I just sat in the back of that small room and didn't say anything. But the whole time, I was looking at the people onstage, thinking, *I can do that.* It was my first glimmer of hope. I mean, I wasn't delusional. When I'd watch Chris Rock or Jerry Seinfeld, I'd think, *I could never do that.* But watching open-mic night? For *sure* I could do that! The third time I went there, I told the old lady who was holding the clipboard that I wanted to sign up. She put on her glasses, looked down at the paper, and said, "Okay, come back Wednesday, June 24th. We have a spot for you that night. You can do two minutes."

At that point, June 24 was nearly a month away, and for that entire stretch, I was a nervous wreck. I felt sick. I didn't want to eat. I couldn't sleep. I would wake up in the middle of the night sweating. When the night finally came, I got up there and shuffled to the mic stand. I still remember my first joke: "I don't know if you noticed, but my skin is kind of dark. In the summer, I get very tan and people always ask me what race I am. I tell them, 'I'm not white. I'm more like wheat.'" ZERO LAUGHS. I was shook. I had come from telling jokes in church, where they *always* laughed. I followed up nervously. "Well, my dad's white, but my mom is nine-grain." Even worse. The silence was deafening. Look, it's not a great joke, and my whole two minutes didn't go over well at all. In fact, it's fair to say that

I bombed. But I remember driving home that night in my silver Honda Civic and thinking, *This is what I'm going to do for the rest of my life*. I was obsessed with it. The energy, the feelings, the rush. It was like nothing I had ever experienced. I was completely hooked. And looking back on it, that's the crazy thing. Because I failed. Miserably. But I wanted to try it again. Immediately.

It was two weeks before they'd let me onstage again, and I'm not sure I did that much better the second time, but I kept going. As much as they'd let me onstage, I'd get up there. The weird thing was, I was living at home at the time but wouldn't tell my parents where I was going all those nights. It was another secret. At dinner, they'd ask me where I was headed or where I had been the night before, and I'd just say, "I can't tell you." I have no idea what they thought was going on, but I'm sure they were worried.

Finally, after a couple of months of this, I came clean and told them I'd been doing stand-up comedy. Their minds were totally blown. They couldn't get their heads around it. They were naturally worried about their darling son being in an environment where people were drinking and talking about sex and whatever else, but they also thought it was pretty awesome and wanted to support me. They thought of it like I had been drafted into the NFL, because all they know of comedy is what they had seen on television somewhere. But neither they nor I knew anything about the next four years of open-mic nights at dive bars that I was about to endure.

I didn't really want my parents to come see me perform, but if I was going to really do comedy for the rest of my life, I couldn't hide it from them forever. So one Wednesday night toward the end of that summer, they went with me to open-mic night.

The Laughing Skull is a relatively tiny room, seating maybe seventy people, and it is about as unchristian as you can imagine. It's dark, the floor is sticky with last night's drinks, and I think there were some mannequins of naked women along the walls. Here come my parents, carrying a video camera and draping the extension cord across half the club.

My act was clean, but the guy who went on before me that night was filthy. So, I'm sitting there in back, getting ready to go on, as he's doing a bit that involves having sex while eating Starbursts. I'm just imagining my parents in the audience, recoiling in horror. To their credit, they stuck it out and watched my two minutes—then left immediately after, which is not a good look for the new guy at a comedy club. But in their defense, they live by a certain set of convictions, and if someone or something goes against those convictions, they don't support it. I've always respected them for that. Plus, there was a two-drink minimum at the comedy club, and there are only so many Sprites you can drink. I'm sure the entire experience didn't make them any less worried about the path I'd chosen, but at least they knew what it was.

SCOREBOARD

When I got back to Colorado Springs at the end of the summer, all I wanted to do was tell jokes. The only problem was that the comedy club out there, Loonees, would let me go on and do my two or three minutes of material only once every six or seven weeks. I made my way to Comedy Works in Denver too, which was a big club, and when I could get on there, it was huge. I'd bring only my A-list material. But again, they didn't want to see me more than once every couple of months.

Comedy isn't like playing the piano or painting. You can practice those things in private, and it can be just as valuable as doing them in public. But for stand-up, doing it in front of a mirror or even in front of your buddies just doesn't cut it. You need an audience. So I got in the habit of going wherever I could find one. I'd show up at music open-mic nights and just do jokes, which generally killed, if only because, let's face it, most of the folks who play music open mics are pretty dreadful.

One of my earliest gigs was at an open-mic comedy contest at a Chili's. Seriously. It was down in Pueblo, which was a good ninety-minute drive from Colorado Springs. The thing about a comedy night at a restaurant is this: When people are playing music at some bar and grill, customers can pretty much decide whether or not to pay attention or interact with that music. If you want to carry on talking to your buddy, that's fine. The music just adds to the ambience. With comedy, it's not like that. We're interrupting your conversation. A comedian needs a light on him. He needs a sound system. He needs a crowd that is facing him and waiting to hear what he has to say. This Chili's in Pueblo had none of that.

I remember dragging my friend DJ with me, arriving, and telling this guy in his white Chili's shirt that I was there for the comedy contest. He wrote my name down, and then I just had to kind of wait around in a restaurant that wasn't even half-full. When it was my turn to go up, there wasn't really any "up." There was no stage, and the only sound system was the same grainy ceiling intercom they would use to announce, "Mr. Thomas, party of four, your table is ready."

By the way, stand-up is never really something you want to surprise people with. As I started to tell my first joke, I distinctly remember people looking up from their jalapeño poppers, craning their necks out their booths, glancing at me, and wondering what exactly I was doing. I probably should have been wondering the same thing. It was a really weird scene: Servers kept taking orders, drinks were being poured, and the volume on TVs at the bar were not even lowered. I remember hearing cheering once and thinking, *Yeah, that joke really landed,* only to realize that the cheers were for the Broncos blocking a punt on *Sunday Night Football.*

So, I did my few minutes, and then after three or four other comics had also done the same, the customers were supposed to vote for a winner with their applause. I believe the winner got a free appetizer. Now, I have an issue with judging comedy like this. I mean, if you're doing archery, whoever gets more arrows closest to the bull's-eye wins. If you're running a race, the winner is the person who crosses the finish line first. But comedy is subjective. Everyone's sense of humor is different. Which is maybe just my way of saying that of course I didn't win. I remember the guy who won, Garrett Waller, was from Pueblo and brought his whole family to the restaurant—and he had a *really* big family—so the fix was in. The place exploded for the guy. I just had my buddy DJ.

Oddly enough, as dire as that gig might have been, I still kind of loved it. Maybe I felt alive for the first time in a while or I liked the rush. I don't know, but I would've rather been there than playing softball with my roommates or home watching television or whatever else I might have been doing on a random Sunday night. In fact, I actually went back to do that comedy contest a couple more times. Still never won. Still mad about it.

But around this time, I did actually win one of those comedy shoot-outs. It was at another place in Pueblo, called—and I swear I'm not making this up—the Bar. Just, the Bar. That was the best name they could come up with, I guess. I doubt there were even a dozen people in the place, but I won, and it was the first time I had really ever won anything. After my victory, the host, Charlie, came over and gave me my prize, which I could feel him pass to me as he shook my hand. It was actual money! I felt the crumpled bills as he pressed them into my palm. In my head, I was wondering, *Are they tens? Twenties? Hundreds?* As I walked away, I looked down into my hand and could see that it was three sweaty balled-up one-dollar bills. I headed toward my car, doing the calculations in my head: I had paid a five-dollar cover charge to get into the bar, I'd used about twenty dollars' worth of gas to drive to Pueblo and back, and I had just made three dollars for all my trouble. The thing that many people might struggle to understand is that this did not upset me. Not in the slightest. In fact, the thrill of that victory was no less sweet than selling out the Ryman in Nashville or getting a standing ovation at the Fox Theatre in Atlanta or getting ten million views on a thirty-second YouTube video imagining if soccer and golf announcers switched jobs. These are just the world's different ways of telling me the thing I've always been dying to hear: "Hey, dude, we see you. You're funny. You matter."

CRAZY IN LOVE

They say that comedy comes from pain and heartbreak, and for me, anyway, that's definitely true. I don't mean this metaphorically either.

I met the first girl I've ever really thought I was in love with in Kenya. To clarify: She was a girl from our church. I know that's a letdown. How cool would it have been to find out my first real girlfriend was from the Maasai tribe? That she taught me how to hunt for food and I taught her how to post Instagram stories? That she taught me how to grow vegetables in the Kenyan soil and I taught her about the wonders of Axe body spray?

No, we were on a mission trip through our church in Colorado Springs when I met Jess. I was one of the leaders of the mission team, so it was my responsibility to make sure everyone was all set before bed. On that particular night, I was told to bring a mattress to one of the female dorms because they were one short. I knocked on the door, someone opened it, and Jess was sitting on the top bunk. Her hair was wet because she'd just showered, and I made some kind of joke about that. She laughed and I liked her instantly.

Jess was gorgeous and clearly way out of my league. She was kind of the church's "It girl": Every guy there seemed to be obsessed with her. She was cool and funny and confident in herself. I liked that. I made her laugh, and we became friends but nothing more than that initially. I knew she didn't like me as much as I liked her. I was *way* into her.

Jess and I hung out a lot, but gradually it became more difficult for me to just be her friend. The more I saw of her, the more I wanted to see of her and be with her. We would maybe go to dinner or a movie, but then the next night, I wouldn't be with her and all I could think about was who she was with and what she was doing. We'd be on her couch watching a movie, and I'd hear her phone vibrate and see texts come in to her phone from guys named Nick and Matt. I'd wonder, *Who the heck is Nick, and what does he want at midnight?* But I wasn't her boyfriend, so I knew I wasn't allowed to ask, and that drove me crazy. (Yes, this is very unhealthy. I am aware.)

I knew something had to change. Finally, I got up the nerve and asked her to be my girlfriend. This was not just the first time I asked *her* to be my girlfriend; this was the first time I'd asked *anyone*. I was twenty-five! I laid it all out for her, was vulnerable, put my feelings on display. She listened closely, heard my heartfelt proposal, and shrugged. "Nah, I'm good." I wasn't deterred. Remember, the whole not-scared-of-rejection thing? A few weeks later, I asked again. She said no again. I was disappointed but had convinced myself I could not live without this girl. In February 2010 right around Valentine's Day, I decided to go for broke.

At the time, I had an entry-level cubicle job doing sales and I had done a few open-mic nights, but everything felt a little lost and directionless. I know—who could turn this guy down? Right, ladies? Anyway, I had gotten obsessed with Jess and convinced myself that she, and she alone, was the thing that was going to sort my life out.

My buddy Louis, the same college roommate who introduced me to the joys of Cedric the Entertainer, insisted I take a different approach with her this time. He was sick of me calling him and crying, er, complaining about how in love I was with this girl. So he told me, "All right, dude, this is what you're gonna do: Tell her that either she's going to date you or you can't be friends with her anymore." I know this sounds like a terrible idea, but in comparison to my other idea—to tell her that God came to me in a dream and said we have to be together—it actually sounded reasonable. The fact that Louis was also a twenty-five-year-old single guy himself with no particular expertise with women probably should have given me pause. It didn't. I went forward with Louis's plan, and the strangest thing happened: It worked!

Immediately, I started investing every ounce of energy into this relationship. I stopped going out to comedy clubs because I just wanted to hang with Jess all the time. The only things I cared about were looking at her and being around her. We hung out; we watched sports; I took her to Texas Roadhouse once. What more could a woman ask for?

I was certain that she was the girl for me. And for a while, it was amazing. But it doesn't take a psychologist to recognize that this level of fixation is not healthy. I was always pushing for more and more relationship commitment from her. I would tell her that she'd saved my life, that I couldn't imagine being without her. I can look back on it now and see that that was way too much pressure to put on any one person. I can look back on it now and see that no human being could give the amount of affirmation and love I needed. I was asking her to fill a twenty-five-year deficit in a few months. She genuinely liked me, but this was not a partnership of equals.

It should come as no surprise to anyone who has ever been in a relationship what happened next: That November, nine months after we started dating, Jess called me over and told me she couldn't do it anymore, that she was breaking up with me.

It was earth shattering. She was pretty broken up about it, but I was destroyed. Absolutely devastated. I cried. A lot. We've all been there, despondent and not knowing if or how the world will ever continue. (Spoiler alert: It will.) I started acting like a crazy person. I'd drive by her house at night to see if there were any cars there. One time, I saw her driving and followed her car for a while to see where she was going. (Turns out she was going to Panera Bread.) I can laugh about it now, but there was nothing funny about it at the time. Those same themes—*you are unlovable, no one cares about you*—were hard to miss.

LAUGHTER IS THE BEST MEDICINE

Jess had broken up with me on a Thursday, and by chance, I had two stand-up gigs booked for that weekend. I was so emotionally incapacitated from the breakup that I thought there was simply no way I could possibly get onstage and try to make *other* people laugh when I hadn't stopped crying in forty-eight hours. But I guess somewhere in the back of my head, I could hear the voice of my dad talking about his 4 A.M. milk runs and how a real man never calls in sick to work. So I dragged myself out to the shows and made a startling discovery: Once I got onstage, I felt so free. For just those moments, the pain of rejection melted away. I don't know if it was the endorphin rush of being up there or the affirmation of hearing people laugh at my jokes, but when I had the microphone in my hand, I didn't hurt anymore. Granted, the cure was temporary (I was still thinking like a crazy person for some time while I was offstage), but knowing that I had this refuge from pain onstage changed my focus. Immediately, I started devoting every spare minute I had to comedy. It was cathartic. Soon I was doing three to four shows a night. I am convinced that I got really good at stand-up quickly because of getting dumped. Comedy was my escape from the pain. And the pain was heavy, so I needed an extra-strength dose of stand-up.

I don't think it's an exaggeration to say I became addicted to comedy. The rush I got onstage was physical, it was chemical, and I craved it. So I played any shows that I could. It wasn't just at comedy clubs and churches. I'd play college cafeterias. I played an old strip club that had a comedy show on the dancers' night off. I did comedy at a gay bar, at children's birthdays, at addiction-recovery meetings—literally anyplace where there was a microphone, and a few places where there wasn't. I once did a gig at a crisis-pregnancy center. This is a place where churches direct women who are considering getting an abortion so they can learn about other options. If you think that seems like an awful place to do stand-up, you're wrong.

What I've found is that any place where people are in pain, anyplace where there is tension that needs to be cut, anyplace where there are things everyone is thinking but nobody is saying—those are great places to do comedy. The crisis-pregnancy center was a startlingly good gig. In fact, the worst audiences are where people are comfortable and free of worries. That's why cruise-ship gigs are generally terrible. I've done plenty of them, but a bunch of rich people sitting around relaxing in their visors and deck shoes, drinking piña coladas, is not going to be a warm audience. The audiences on these ships are kinda like "Dance for me, monkey! Entertain me!" whereas at a crisis-pregnancy center or a military base, they're *so* appreciative that you came. Anything to take their minds off everything else going on around them.

My appetite for performing knew no bounds. Once when I was living in Denver, I wanted to get onstage so badly one night that me and a couple of comedian friends got in a car and drove four hours to an open mic at a bar in Wyoming. We got there, and the bartender thought we had lost our minds.

"You drove from Denver to perform at an open mic here?"

"Yeah, we couldn't get on at the club in Denver tonight and this was the closest spot." We were junkies. We couldn't get enough.

THE SECRET HANDSHAKE

Comedy Works in Denver became my home base. It's a great club—Roseanne Barr and Josh Blue both started there—and I went from being an open-mic comic there to being a headliner about as fast as you can possibly do it, which is about four years. I was *that* driven.

Around 2011, when I was still a young comic there, I had worked myself up the ladder far enough that they were letting me host the club's open-mic night on Tuesdays. I can remember one of the first times I hosted, noticing that the club's owner was in the building. This was pretty unusual for an open-mic night—she was rarely even there on the weekends—but I didn't think too much of it until the club's manager pulled me aside backstage.

"Hey, just wanted to let you know, Dave Chappelle is in town, and he's going to drop in and come on tonight."

I immediately started sweating. "What? Dave Chappelle is coming here? To be on the show that I'm hosting?"

A little context: *Chappelle's Show* pretty much changed my life. I used to watch it over and over when I was in college.

Some of those sketches are among the funniest things I've ever seen. He abruptly left the show before the third season started, despite a fifty-million-dollar contract from Comedy Central, and more or less disappeared for a long while, which had the effect of essentially building up his legend. To me, he was not just the biggest star in comedy; he was the biggest star in anything. At the time, he had just started to reemerge from his self-imposed exile. He wasn't touring. He was still basically a man of mystery. The idea that he would be showing up to do open-mic night at a club in Denver was like some kind of comedy second coming or something. The tension was that great.

The club tweeted out something about "a very special guest" stopping by, so suddenly the place began to fill up. Fifty people became 100 and then 250. The place was packed out. By about 9:00 P.M., we had blitzed through all the open mic-ers, but Chappelle hadn't turned up yet. Apparently, he was at dinner and would be along soon. Because, you know, when you're *the* Dave Chappelle, you can do that. So I was told, "We need you to go out there and stretch. Just do some jokes."

Do some jokes? If someone handed me a microphone now, I could probably get onstage and go for an hour or two without a problem. But back then, I had maybe five minutes of material. MAYBE! More to the point, if I was up there before Dave Chappelle, I wanted to be up there murdering. My nightmare would be for him to walk into the club and see me eating it onstage. So I stretched. And stretched. And, surprisingly, I was doing okay. I was cobbling it together. The crowd was laughing. Finally, after maybe fifteen minutes, I saw the guy at the soundboard flash the light to indicate Chappelle was backstage and ready to go. It hit me that he was right behind the curtain, less than five feet from me. My heart was racing, but in the most understated way I could, I simply turned to the crowd and said, "Ladies and gentlemen, we have a special guest tonight. This man needs no introduction. Please give a round of applause for Dave Chappelle."

The place erupted. Standing ovation. Chappelle walked out cradling a beer and smoking a cigarette. *What an absolute legend,* I thought. He put the beer down, gave me one of those half-hug/half-high-five things, and went to work. It was one of the best days of my life. I mean, it's not like I know Chappelle, but there I was, dapping it up with him onstage. There is a kind of fraternity among stand-ups, and this felt like I was being inducted.

MARRIED TO THE GAME

Louie Anderson once told me, "Comedy is your mistress." I think he's right. Every time I'm hanging with friends or at a family reunion or doing anything else, I'm always wondering when I can get out of there and be with comedy. It's crazy. For practically my whole life, whenever I started to get into any sort of relationship, comedy always got in the way. I've had women say to me, "Hey, can you just, like, *not* go to the comedy club for one night?" But I wasn't willing to make comedy secondary in my life. There were times when I was not even performing but just wanted to be at a club so I could be around comedy. Comedians are my people. I've always felt loved by comedians. It was not so much for my material; I just felt accepted and understood by comics in a way that not many other people ever understood me.

Comics prioritize comedy in a way that probably sounds insane to other people. My friend and fellow comedian Tim Hawkins jokes with me sometimes about this: "Yo, I just got a really bad health diagnosis, but I've got this new closer that's killing." I'd nod and say, "Yeah, dude, my life is falling apart, but this new tag on my joke is unbelievable." We're kidding, but also we're not. To me, there's no problem that I've ever encountered that is not solved—at least in the short term—by a hot comedy set. I'm 100 percent serious. A warm crowd, a good set, and you're up there, feeling totally free—it *is* like being on drugs.

A few years after Jess broke up with me, I played a gig opening for a band at Red Rocks, which is a beautiful, iconic venue in Denver. The Beatles and Jimi Hendrix have played there. The Dave Matthews Band and U2 recorded live albums at the place. I'd only been doing stand-up for about three years, and this was one of the biggest crowds I'd ever performed in front of. There were close to ten thousand people there. I crushed it. It was as good a show as I'd ever done up to that point in my career. I had someone take a photo of that show from behind the stage so you could just about see every one of those ten thousand people. And you better believe I posted that photo everywhere I could.

Just by chance, Jess—the very girl who had dumped me—was there that night. I didn't know she was coming, and the last time she'd heard about me doing stand-up, I was basically an open mic-er, so I think she was pretty shocked. She texted me after the show and told me how amazing the show was. Three years earlier, this simple interaction would have had me in my feelings for weeks. But at this point, I was over her. I was in a committed relationship. With comedy.

13

SEXUAL REELING

I was about ten when my dad sat me and my brother Joe down for the Sex Talk. I had heard the word *sex* from my buddy Evan at church, but I didn't know what it meant.

As you can imagine, in an evangelical Christian household, sex was not a frequent topic of discussion. In fact, it was rarely ever mentioned by my parents outside the bounds of this talk. It's funny—the Christian band DC Talk had a song about sex on their album *Free at Last* called "I Don't Want It." It was obviously very anti-sex in its messaging—the gist was "Don't have sex until marriage"—but we weren't even allowed to listen to *that* song. Apparently, anti-sex messaging was still too sexy. Just out of pure habit, I still skip track 14 on *Free at Last* whenever it comes up on my Spotify.

It wasn't just music. When we would watch movies as a family, anytime there was a scene that even hinted at sex, Mom or Dad would dive for the fast-forward button on the remote control quicker than Michael Phelps. It all seems very silly looking back on it now. I remember watching *Braveheart,* a historical epic, and people were getting gored and beheaded right, left, and center. I remember a soldier getting shot in the eye with a bow and arrow. My dad and I high-fived. But when a husband made love to his wife, before going off to defend her honor at war, it was considered a shocking breach of family values. Or how about *Titanic*? The idea of people leaping to their deaths or babies freezing in the North Atlantic was okay, but the minute Kate Winslet took off her shirt, my parents were ready to burn the DVD in our front yard. A tricky way to grow up, I'll tell you that.

So, my earliest introductions to the topic of sex were served up with a side of shame. Sex was dirty. It was bad. Except within the bounds of marriage, for procreation, when it's wonderful and it glorified God. Which, as you might imagine, could all be a bit confusing for a kid.

Remember the *Lion King*? Mufasa points out the Shadowlands to Simba. "What's that over there?" "That is Sex, Simba. We don't ever, ever go there." Well, that was my sex education in a nutshell—that and Dad's big talk.

It is kind of surreal to recall. My dad called me and my brother up to a new wing of our house where he was doing some minor construction at the time and told us to sit on the bed. I think he was more nervous and uncomfortable talking about it than me and my brother were. He kept everything very scientific and matter-of-fact. There was no talk of pornography or masturbation or anything like that. This was more like a biology lecture. But with props! He brought along two soccer trophies—each with a soccer player on the top of it—to help him illustrate the mechanics of sex. For real. As my dad was, uh, orchestrating these two trophies together, my thinking was totally clear: *I'm never doing that. Never in a million years. Why would anyone ever even want to?*

I was really a very innocent kid. I can remember going to an evangelical church camp one summer out in Alabama. This was real middle-of-nowhere, Deep South, redneck country, and this camp was steeped in the charismatic Christian traditions. So in addition to swimming and archery and kayaking and all the other typical summer-camp stuff, you'd have praise-and-worship time, prayer time, and that sort of thing. At prayer time, kids would come forward to ask Jesus into their hearts or to receive help for some sort of issue they were having.

At one point, me and my older brother Barton came forward to get prayer. Everyone was doing it, so I guess we figured we would too. A woman who was a leader in our church at the time started praying for me and my brother. I will never forget what she said.

"Dear God, bless these beautiful children," she began. "Keep them safe. Steer them toward the path of righteousness." That was all pretty standard, but then her prayer veered down a very odd path. "We just ask that you'd break the spirit of masturbation in their lives."

Uhh, what? My brother and I both opened our eyes and stole a glance at each other. *What was she talking about?* At that point, I didn't even know what masturbation was. So, of course, it came up on the car ride home from camp with my parents. My mom was furious!

"Where did you learn that? This is a Christian camp. Who are these bad-influence kids you are hanging out with?"

"Um, it was our youth leader . . . during prayer."

◼ LEAVING THE (CENTER)FOLD

Everything was strict and well-mannered in my family when I was a kid. Anything remotely sexual was forbidden. So when I was growing up, real information about sex and sexuality wasn't really available to me (the Shadowland, Simba, the Shadowland). It was something I had to sort of piece together myself through whatever little scraps of information I stumbled across. Sometimes literally.

Back then, there was an area near my house that we called the Mud Flats, where my brothers and I used to ride our dirt bikes. It was basically an old construction site where we'd built some dirt jumps and ramps for our bikes. Typical neighborhood-boy stuff. One day we were riding there and I looked down to my left and saw an old issue of *Playboy* just sitting there, half-open, with a naked woman staring back at us from the page. Our minds were completely blown. We had no context for that. None of us had ever seen such a thing. For a split second, we just froze, unsure of what to do. It's another one of those childhood moments that I remember like it was yesterday. We jumped back on our bikes and pedaled home as fast as we could. It was almost as if this naked centerfold was chasing us home. We were genuinely frightened of her. We knew it was bad even though we didn't know why. We clattered into the house, huffing and puffing, and the first person we saw was my mom.

"Hey, kids," she said. "Why are you all so out of breath?

Silence.

More silence.

"We were just racing at the Mud Flats," I said.

We never told her about the *Playboy*. It wasn't as if we'd even done anything wrong, but it certainly felt like we had. It was like Adam and Eve in the garden. We felt that shame. We had *looked*. We felt exposed. We had something to hide now.

I remember lying in bed that night, thinking about it. I could not get that *Playboy* out of my head. It was scary. It was bad. And I *had* to see it again. So the next day, I kind of suggested to my brothers that we should go back to the Mud Flats to ride bikes. Once we were there, I stole another peek at the *Playboy* when they weren't looking. Just like that, the guilt and the lying and the hiding had begun.

I grew up consumed with shame about any sexual thoughts or impulses I had. When I was about eleven or twelve, me and my buddies would sneak out of church and go to the Denny's parking lot across the street, where we'd call 1-900 sex-talk hotlines from the pay phone. We would never even get past this sensual voice on the other end of the line saying hello before we would immediately hang up. We couldn't handle it. I'm sure this is the kind of thing that lots of kids that age would've done—at least in the era when there were pay phones and 1-900 hotlines—but I thought this made me some kind of sexual deviant.

It wasn't just my parents who were making me feel this way; it was the evangelical world I was surrounded by. Girls who wore shirts to school that didn't cover a bra strap would be made to wear choir robes all day or a big, oversized "shirt of shame." If they wore short skirts, they were considered sluts. If they made out with a boyfriend, it was even worse. Somehow so much anxiety and shame about sex got channeled into dress codes. I've heard stories from other people about getting in trouble for wearing hair gel or an outlawed shade of nail polish or body lotion that was too shimmery. A woman told me that all the girls in her school were expected to put Band-Aids over their nipples when it was cold. Another told me that her church made kids wear jeans to go swimming in the ocean because swimsuits were scandalous. In some Christian schools, boys were not allowed to wear pink. Don't even get me started on that. All this stuff is funny to recount, but, trust me, it leaves a mark.

In high school, I went to an accountability group, where we had to confess each week if we had seen nudity in movies or stared too long at a Victoria's Secret catalog or had impure thoughts about Pamela Anderson while watching *Baywatch*. I remember my buddy confessing that he had sexual thoughts about a girl he saw at the pool. We all gathered around and prayed for him. This is all very wild to recall because *now* it feels like a comedy bit, like this is part of my stand-up show. But at the time, it was very real and very serious. If any of us had thoughts about sex, we were kind of made to feel like addicts or monsters, when in fact we were all pretty good kids.

Fear and shame remained my primary emotions when it came to anything remotely sexual. When I was about seventeen, my friend Isaac and I were on spring break with his family, playing golf at a course right by a condominium complex. Two girls were looking down on us from the second-floor balcony of one of the condos. When we looked back at them, one of them flashed us. I was shocked. I had never seen anything like that before. In fact, my reaction wasn't much different from when I'd seen the pages of that *Playboy* at the Mud Flats years earlier. I froze. No one had ever taught me how to handle that type of situation! Again, I'm telling this story and you're imagining me being twelve or thirteen. No! I was about to graduate high school!

"Hey, let's go up there and meet them," Isaac said to me.

I was terrified of that idea.

"We're not gonna kiss them, are we?" I asked in all my teenage innocence.

Isaac still makes fun of me to this day for that line. Anytime we're together and I see a woman, he's like, "You're not going to kiss her, are you?"

To be fair, at that point in my life, I'd never kissed a girl. Matter of fact, it would be years before I finally did. I made it through four years of college—and plenty of unbelievably awkward moments with girls who were certainly expecting me to kiss them—without registering my first real kiss. When I finally did, I was twenty-two years old. *Twenty-two!* At that point, toward the end of college, I'd met someone and we had started unofficially dating. She was leaving for a summer internship, and we went out for breakfast the morning she was leaving. Afterward, we kissed by my car. It was all very innocent—I cared about her and was going to miss her—and it was kind of amazing. It actually felt spiritual in a way. I wasn't trying to do anything scandalous, I just had sincere feelings toward her. Afterward, I didn't feel any shame about it. I was proud, in fact. I felt like a real man! Thus adding to the confusion. My fear of sex didn't exactly recede after that.

In my twenties, when I started dating Jess, whom I really loved and thought I was going to marry, the physical side of our relationship was a minefield. One night, after we were making out on her couch, I freaked out. I loved being close to her, I was incredibly attracted to her, but all those thoughts made me feel like I was doing something wrong.

"I've got to go talk to the pastor," I told her.

She was confused. I was a mess. By the time she broke up with me, I was twenty-six. Shame had overcome me and I'd never even seen her naked.

Looking back, I guess I put sex on some sort of pedestal. (Maybe I should blame Dad's trophy-assisted intro to the subject for that.) I had always been taught in church that the way to show love and respect for a woman you really cared about was *not* to have sex with her. Sex was the glue to bind a marriage together, but outside of that, it had no place. Most of the women I dated, though, were confused by these kinds of ideas. When I was starting to tour around the country, I met a woman in Las Vegas and we hit it off. I liked her a lot. She was different from anybody I'd ever dated before. We laughed and had fun together, but when we started dating, she couldn't understand why I didn't want to have sex with her.

"Aren't you attracted to me?" she asked me one night, upset. "Don't you think I'm hot?"

I was and I did. I tried to explain how I was raised to believe that I was honoring her by abstaining from having sex with her. It was a sign of respect.

"Not to me," she said. After I explained it, at least she understood where I was coming from, but I know it was hard for her to deal with. It was all very confusing to her, and her confusion was confusing to me. That's a lot of confusion. In the end, it was a whole jumbled mess.

Here's what I do know: Looking back at my sex "education," or lack thereof, all the confusion and shame led me to create a sort of secret life for myself, and not a cool secret life where I was a mild-mannered stand-up by day and a fearless caped crime fighter by night. In public, I was being lauded by Christians and performing comedy at churches, but in private, I was doing things that I knew would not go down well in that world: drinking, looking at porn, making out—and sometimes more than that—with women. Pretty average behavior for a single comedian in his thirties, but I knew the church world wouldn't approve. The secrecy not only made me feel terrible about it but also built up a gigantic fear of what would ever happen to me if my secrets were exposed, which, in turn, only pushed me to try even harder to hide it all.

14

TRUST ME—I WATCHED A DOCUMENTARY

During the last election, I walked out of the polling place and was handed a colorful sticker with the phrase "I Voted" in big block letters. They've been giving these things out for a while now, but it was the first time I really started to think hard about those little stickers. What are they really for? I know I voted, so I don't really need the sticker as a reminder of what happened in my life forty-five seconds earlier. No, it is to let *the world* know that I voted. I'm supposed to put that sticker proudly on my shirt so everyone can know I've done my civic duty, so people will look at me with more respect. Maybe they'll see that sticker and feel so impressed that they'll go right out and vote too. That's a good thing, I think. I mean, we definitely want our elections decided by people who are convinced to vote by seeing a stranger wearing a sticker on their shirt. That's democracy at work!

(Steps up onto imaginary soapbox.)

Look, it's your civic *duty* to vote. Basically, it is your job if you live in this country and are a citizen and haven't murdered people. (Those are the voting qualifications, right?) With that in mind, flaunting your "I Voted" sticker, posting it on Facebook or Instagram, feels a bit like a millennial participation trophy. What, it wasn't enough that the people at the supermarket saw that you voted? You need all your relatives, your friends from high school, that weird guy you used to work with, and your kind-of-racist uncle to know too? It's not like voting is *that* hard. You went and stood in line. Then you pushed some buttons on a touch screen. Or maybe you just filled out a ballot and mailed it in. It's not like you just marched across the bridge in Selma or stormed the beaches in Normandy. The people who did that can get a sticker. But for voting? Maybe just do it and get on with the rest of your day, okay?

(Steps off soapbox and takes deep breath.)

Okay, I'm chill. I'm chill.

But for real, isn't there a point when bragging about your good deeds kind of negates the point of doing them in the first place? I imagine there has always been an element of charity, philanthropy, and general do-gooderism that has been overly concerned with public perception. I mean, people have been putting their names on university buildings and cancer centers for a *really* long time. But social media has exacerbated this to such an extent that doing good is no longer the end in itself. If no one sees you do good, it's like that proverbial tree falling in a forest: It might as well have never happened.

My Facebook and Instagram feeds are filled with photos of people acting virtuous. But how do you think that homeless guy feels when you insist on taking a photo of yourself giving him a hamburger? I mean, I'm sure he's happy for the food, but are we now insisting that the price of that burger for him is to become a prop on your ongoing quest to convince the world of your inherent decency?

The fixation on looking like better people than we actually are did not start with social media. At least not for me. Samford, where I went to college, was a Christian school, so on Sunday mornings, everyone was supposed to go to church, and then all the students would go to the school cafeteria right afterward, still wearing their Sunday best. To show up to the Samford cafeteria on a Sunday afternoon in shorts and a T-shirt was to broadcast to the whole university that you were a bad Christian, that you didn't go to church. So often on Sundays, I'd sleep in, roll out of bed, take a shower, get dressed up in my church clothes, then roll into the Samford cafeteria and blend right in. Mind you, I didn't invent this little ruse. Lots of people did it.

GOOD IRL

I was at a church in Indiana not too long ago and noticed they had something called "alternate giving cards" in all the seats. I had never seen these before, so I asked someone who worked at the church what they were.

"Well, many people choose to give their money to the church online."

"Yes. And?"

"Well, when we were passing the basket around, they were feeling very self-conscious that other people were noticing them not dropping cash or a check into the basket. So this way, people will know that you give online."

Face, meet palm.

I mean, look, I totally understand the impulse. Reread the

section above: I'm the guy that would put on church clothes for lunch so people would think I went to church beforehand. We're cut from the very same cloth! Millions of Christians across the globe are being persecuted and killed because of their faith in Jesus, but American Christians are so concerned with how others are perceiving them that they need a little pat on the back, me included. Kind of embarrassing.

You see the same thing with mission trips. I mean, really, what's the point of going on a mission trip without letting everyone in the airport know of your humanitarian sacrifices by wearing matching fluorescent T-shirts that read, "First Baptist Church—Colombia 2018—Doing the Lord's Work." Lest I sound judgmental, please know that I have donned plenty of those garish T-shirts myself over the years.

When we used to go on elementary school field trips, we all had to wear matching shirts so we wouldn't get lost or separated from one another. But frequently it's groups of otherwise perfectly capable adults sporting their identical mission trip gear. Why? Are we hoping that everyone waiting in line to go through security will get to see what great people we are? Do we want the TSA agents to thank us? I mean, I've been on a lot of mission trips. It seems that every person who goes on one has the same goal: to get photos with minority kids to post on social media. Oh, and also to do the Lord's work. Don't worry: If you scroll back far enough on my Instagram, you can see that I've done this one too.

Here's the thing: For many Christians living in the twenty-first century, going on a mission trip is a very important rite of passage in their lives. It represents, unequivocally, the absolute apex moment for tagging themselves on social media. Think about it: You're in a strange, often exotic locale (a chance for really good photos!) doing something that is supposed to help other people (a chance for amazing virtue signaling!). Sadly, sometimes that seems to be the whole point.

I went on a mission trip to Honduras once, and we were supposed to go down there and build a bathhouse. But when we got to the site one day, it had just rained, so the ground was soft and we couldn't start work. There was really nothing for us to do there that day. You want to know what we did? We moved a bunch of cinder blocks around the construction site and took photos of ourselves doing it so we could document the toil and sweat we were putting into this wonderful charitable project. Never mind that those cinder blocks *did not need to be moved.* Here's the worst part: We left the site that day feeling great. We'd worked hard for no purpose beyond documenting the fact that we were working hard. Although, to be fair, I *did* have a few blisters on my hands, and my arms were sore for a week. But don't worry about me—I got a massage in the airport terminal on our way home.

Look, it's certainly possible to be really cynical about mission trips, but I believe there are tangible benefits to these excursions. It's just that they aren't necessarily the same benefits that the organizers of the trips have in mind. Taking sheltered white kids from America and showing them how people in other parts of the world live is valuable and eye opening. Sometimes missionaries build real relationships with locals in the places they visit. That is even more valuable, maybe even worth the few thousand dollars that most of these trips cost. I remember playing soccer with some street kids in Egypt once, and afterward their parents explained, through a translator, that they really appreciated that we'd fly halfway around the world to see them. They felt valued by us, that their lives mattered. That's real and that made an impact on me. After all, that's the same feeling I've been chasing my whole life too. We all want to be seen and feel like we matter. But the actual work done on mission trips? The evangelizing? Maybe there's someone out there doing it the right way. I just haven't seen many examples of it.

BETTER THAN YOU

That forward-facing, performative vibe kind of infiltrates everything these days, doesn't it? When I wake up in the morning, I don't necessarily put a ton of thought into what I'm going to put on. My main thoughts are, *Do these clothes look okay? Are they comfortable?* and *Are they clean?* For me, that's about as much thinking as I can do before breakfast. But these days, there is this idea that what you're wearing has to *mean* something. Everybody's outfit must have a purpose. I asked a friend recently, "Hey, where did you get that shirt?"

"This T-shirt was made by orphans in third-world countries, operating entirely on solar power, using sustainably sourced cotton. The profits go to Save the Earth. Where did you get your hoodie?"

"Uh, um, Target."

I mean, I get not wanting to buy shoes that were cobbled by illegal child labor, but do all our clothes really need to line up with our political beliefs? Can I sometimes just wear a pair of jeans because I like the way they fit? I think it's great that companies such as Bombas and TOMS donate a pair of socks or shoes to people who need them whenever someone buys a pair, but does that mean if I buy a pair of Nikes, I'm heartless? I am?

Okay, cool. It all just seems like yet another way for someone to boast about what a virtuous soul they are or, worse, an emotional ruse to make consumers feel better about buying another pair of shoes that they probably don't need. One time I told a joke about buying a pair of TOMS. In the joke, I didn't like the shoes and they sat in my closet for a month before I returned them. "I felt bad because TOMS had to send their rep back to Guatemala to get the donated pair back from this kid who was playing soccer in them." I got crushed for that joke. People were genuinely mad at me about it. It was as if TOMS was such a righteous company, such a sacred cow, that merely poking fun at their altruism was somehow out of bounds.

I was at McDonald's recently, and the kid at the register asked me if I'd like to donate money to prevent childhood obesity. "Excuse me, sir, do you care about children?" *I'm in a McDonald's buying a Double Quarter Pounder meal—I quite obviously barely care about myself.* But this happens everywhere we go now. CVS wants me to donate a dollar to save the planet. Kroger wants a dollar for diabetes. I've got to be honest: Sometimes I just want to make a retail transaction without being confronted by the world's ills and my own failings as a human. I was walking through an outdoor mall not that long ago and was accosted by a lady with a clipboard. "Do you have two minutes to save a life?" I mean, what *possible* right answer is there to that question?

There are certain causes that people defend almost reflexively. Look, I'll admit, sometimes I tweet things without thinking that hard about it. And by sometimes, I mean lots of times. Last year over Christmas, I tweeted, "Yo, those Salvation Army bells are loud and annoying. Am I officially the worst person ever? I am? Okay, cool." In my mind, I was thinking, *Surely, other people can relate to this.* And sure enough, they did. Lots of likes and retweets.

"Yes! I've been thinking that for weeks but didn't want to tell anyone!"

"Borderline seizure causing!"

Good, everyone agrees. But then the comments section turned.

"Helping needy people is annoying?"

"Probably not as annoying as being homeless."

"Annoying? The Salvation Army is a CHURCH. The Bell reminds US, the FREE, ABLE, & GRATEFUL, to be JOYFUL GIVERS! Ring in Food! Ring in Shelter! Ring in Hope for Someone's Tomorrow!!"

"Those bells have done more for the kingdom than most people do in five lifetimes!"

"Those bells helped serve over 140,000 individuals here in Columbus, Ohio, through food pantries, utility/rent assistance, after-school programming, drug & alcohol rehabilitation, anti-human-trafficking programs, job training, and spiritual enrichment. Nothing annoying about that!"

You get the picture. Mind you, I wasn't suggesting that the Salvation Army didn't do good work in the community; I was just gently calling out something that everyone was thinking but no one was saying. I wasn't taking any sort of principled stand against the Salvation Army or its volunteers. I mean, could there possibly be a way that they could help feed the homeless or run job-assistance programs without those loud, clanging bells? Maybe. Regardless, people on Twitter jumped at the chance to signal to the world what wonderful, kindhearted, loving people they all were by taking me out behind the digital woodshed and beating me senseless. Happy holidays, I guess.

I'M AN EXPERT

Social media has become a force multiplier for all our worst instincts. It's almost as if real-life interactions have become secondary to online ones. My buddy Mike told me he was at the gym and watched a woman walk in, start the treadmill, then let it run on high for twelve minutes while she sat next to it staring at her phone. When it was finished, she took a photo of the treadmill's screen that showed how far she had "run" and posted it immediately to her Instagram account. That is really an incredible, innovative new way to get in shape. Just think about it: Twelve minutes a day, no sweating, no new workout clothes to buy, no expensive classes at the gym. And if you correctly utilize the photo filters on your Instagram, you can make it look like your new workout is really doing the trick, slimming you down and sculpting your abs, calves, and glutes. The only thing is, you're going to have to avoid *ever* seeing any of your social media followers in person, where they might notice a few of the minor drawbacks of your new fitness regimen. That is incredible, and not in a good way. You're trying to prove to some random people on the internet that you're getting in shape? Why? What exactly is the point of *pretending* to get in shape? And isn't there an easier way to lie about it? Perhaps the most troubling aspect of this whole incident was that she was shamelessly willing to do it in public, in order to get some perceived bump on social media. But then again, Mike posted her doing that to *his* social media, so I'm not really quite sure who is to blame here.

Everybody everywhere has become so desperate to show the world what a noble creature they are. It drives me to all insanity. I guess at a certain point, letting everyone know about your exercise routine became more important than your actual exercise routine. But every time you tell me about your "leg day" or the hour you spend each night on the rowing machine doesn't make me like you more; it just makes me like me less. When I pull up behind your Lexus at a stoplight, I really don't want to see your "26.2" bumper sticker. I've got a sausage biscuit on my lap. It's the same type of feeling we have waking up hungover and seeing the woman posting her open Bible next to a cup of fresh fruit. I already feel bad about myself. I don't need to see your St. Simons Island bumper sticker either. I get it: You run marathons and you're rich. Fantastic. Can't that be enough for you to be happy without having to broadcast it to the world?

A few years ago, we started selling bumper stickers through my website and at shows for people who are willing to be more honest with themselves. One has the dreaded 26.2 on it in big script, and then in parentheses and smaller letters, it reads "Oreos I Can Eat in One Sitting." Another says "13.1 Hours (My Longest Netflix Binge)." They're probably our most popular pieces of merch ever. People love them, and when I see them on people's cars, it makes me so, so happy. Because deep down, I believe people know the truth—the truth about themselves and the truth about humanity.

Speaking of Netflix binges, I read somewhere recently that we are in the "Golden Age of Documentaries." Netflix and all these streaming services have been great for documentary makers because these films that previously would have struggled to get into theaters can now reach millions of people easily. I love that. But, by extension, we are now also in the "Golden Age of Annoying People Who Watch Documentaries." It used to be that in order to become an expert in a subject, you'd go to school, do research, work your way up in the field, undergo extensive training courses, consult with other experts, go back to school, then maybe write a book about it. It was a process that took many years, if not decades. Now we've cut all that down to about ninety minutes. I suppose it's a credit to these filmmakers that everyone who watches *Blackfish* suddenly feels qualified to talk about the crimes of SeaWorld and the emotional lives of killer whales or that everyone who watches *RBG* feels confident explaining gender inequality and intricacies of the Supreme Court, but perhaps a little humility is in order. It's great that your interest has been sparked by this enthralling film, but please at least read a couple of books before giving us your TED Talk.

That old saying "A little knowledge is a dangerous thing" has become more true than it ever was, because now anyone with a smartphone has "a little knowledge" at their fingertips. The internet has turned us all into annoying know-it-alls. Skimming a Wikipedia page does not qualify us to lecture anyone about anything. The result of all this is that knowledge and expertise themselves have become grossly devalued. It used to be that politicians would fight over how to interpret the opinions of experts. They'd argue about what the facts meant. Now they just make up their own facts to fit their opinions. If Wikipedia doesn't agree, that's okay—we can edit it. Whatever nonsense you're spouting, someone somewhere on the internet will surely back you up.

15

LADIES AND GENTLEMEN, JOHN CRIST!

Comedy is a tricky thing, but the premise of good comedy is very simple: You take ideas and thoughts that people can't say or are too afraid to say or that society has told you *not* to say, and you say them. It's really that simple. I guess I was always suited to become a comedian because I was never good with rules just for the sake of rules.

At my Christian high school, there was a rule that you had to keep your shirt tucked in at all times. That was the rule, hard and fast. No exceptions. I had a problem with that. I must have gotten thirty write-ups, a few detentions, and even an in-school suspension or two just for not following that rule. I hated it so much. I didn't understand why we needed to keep our shirts tucked in. Why was that so important? Did Jesus always tuck in his shirt? Not in the pictures I've seen. Look, not bringing a weapon to school—that rule made sense. No lighting fireworks in the gym—I can get on board with that. Seems reasonable. But rules just for the sake of rules always drove me nuts.

I did an internship for a Christian organization called Focus on the Family in Colorado Springs after college. At the time I moved out there, I was twenty-three and had never tasted alcohol before or even had an interest in doing so. But when I got there, they had a rule that no one enrolled in the internship was allowed to drink alcohol, even if we were of legal drinking age. So you know what I did? I immediately went with my two friends Ashley and Monica to Rock Bottom Brewery and tasted my first sip of beer. Isn't that wild? I had literally no desire to drink until someone told me I couldn't. Go figure.

I think that drive to do the thing that I'm not supposed to do has served me well as a comic. Back in 2015, I was at Jr's Last Laugh Comedy Club in Erie, Pennsylvania, opening for Louie Anderson. I had come up with a joke, and before the show, I told Louie about it and how I was nervous to tell it. In that case, he told me I absolutely *had* to tell it. He said that even if the joke failed miserably, I'd be proud of myself for telling it. During Thursday night's show, I couldn't get up the courage to tell it. Friday night, I chickened out again. Finally, Saturday night, I knew I'd be bummed out on the plane ride that I'd let fear get the best of me, so I took the stage and ran through ten or fifteen minutes of my more polished material, finished a bit with a big laugh, and then started in. My heart was practically beating out of my chest.

"I was at a show the other day, and a guy was drinking a Mudslide," I told the audience. "I started thinking, we're so ignorant and arrogant as Americans, we have alcoholic drinks named after the natural disasters of other countries. Like, go to India and order a Mudslide. It wiped out a whole village two weeks ago, but you're going to drink a Mudslide? Very offensive! It's like going to Ireland and ordering a Car Bomb. The bartender just starts crying and says, 'My grandpa died in one.'"

The audience was laughing hard. I pushed the joke further.

"You don't see people in foreign countries ordering drinks of American disasters. How upset would you be if you were sitting in a bar and some European dude sits down and orders a Hurricane Katrina? It's thirteen ounces of alcohol in a twelve-ounce glass. It comes with an umbrella, but it's flipped over. FEMA comes to clean up the mess, but they're three months late."

The crowd was with me. They were howling. I kept going.

"Pretty soon you're going to be in the bar and order a Barack Obama. That's where you order a drink you can't afford and the guy next to you pays for it."

Even bigger laughs. To be fair, I knew that whole section of the joke would work. It was the next line that I was deathly scared to tell. But I pushed forward.

"Or what about someone ordering a Ferguson Police Department? 'What's that?' 'It's six shots in the back.'"

That was just a few months after the police shooting in Ferguson, Missouri. The timing made it feel like the riskiest bit I'd ever done onstage at that point but people—all people, Black, White, whatever—laughed. And they laughed hard. The audience was losing it. And it's because the joke was poking at the things that people were thinking about but afraid to say. It felt like a relief to those people in the club. It wasn't making fun of a tragic death. It wasn't racist. It was simply stating that whatever side or stance or angle or opinion you had on the events that took place in Ferguson the year before, we can *all* agree that it was a disaster. That's it.

A few years ago, I got asked to host the Catalyst conference. At the time, it was the biggest Christian conference in the country. More than ten thousand church leaders and Christians from all across the country would come to Atlanta, Georgia, to gather in an arena to hear from thought leaders, pastors, and visionaries in the Christian community. And they asked me to host! It was a big deal, and I was ready! I remember buying a new outfit for this particular performance—something that, prior to that date, I'd never done. This was my Super Bowl.

I found out that my opening set—kind of like the monologue that opens the Oscars or something—would be ten minutes and I'd be introducing the leader of the whole event, Andy Stanley. Andy is the pastor of one of the biggest churches in America. At the time, though, he was kind of going through a tough time publicly. He had gotten in some hot water from the conservative Christian community for allegedly watering down his messages. They accused him of being more of a motivational speaker than a truth-speaking pastor. Everyone was talking about it in hush-hush terms, but no one would dare say anything aloud about it, especially not at *his* conference.

But what good is a comedian if he doesn't say a word about the greatest and most sensitive issue at hand? So I wrote a joke about it but didn't tell anyone about it and didn't rehearse it because I knew if I did, the producers would cut it. When the time came, they introduced me and I walked onstage and started into my monologue. I was killing. There were roars of laughter through the arena. It felt great. As I started into the joke that came right before the Andy Stanley joke, I could feel my heart starting to beat faster. If I wanted to bail out, I certainly could have. This was my last chance. But I decided to charge forward. As the laughter settled from the previous joke, I took a short pause and a deep breath.

"Man, performing at this conference is great," I started. "I was doing my morning Bible reading backstage, and so many people came by and introduced themselves. Beth Moore stopped by, saw me reading the Bible, and said, 'Oh, John 4—that's one of my favorite passages.' John Piper walked by and said, 'Oh, the NIV—that's my favorite translation.' Then Andy Stanley walked by and said, 'What is that, a Bible? Never heard of it.'"

The arena exploded. Now, I'd like to tell you that it exploded with laughter, but that wouldn't be the whole truth. Certainly, there were a lot of people laughing. But there were also tons of expressions of surprise, lots of looking around like, "Did he really just say that?" Still to this day, people come up to me in airports and churches and tell me they were there when I made that joke. Of course, there were a lot of complaints, a lot of emails to the conference saying the joke was across the line and inappropriate. But Andy pulled me aside afterward and told me he thought that joke was one of the funniest things he'd ever heard. It felt good for him for the same reason it felt good for everyone else in there who laughed: It pointed out the elephant in the room that everyone was trying to ignore, and in doing so, it punctured all that tension. Comedy had won its job that day.

QUALITY TIMING

Comedy is all about timing. I'm hardly the first person to point that out, but that doesn't make it less true. How long do you pause before you hit an audience with a punch line? How long do you let the crowd laugh before you hit them with another joke? What joke do you open with? What do you close with? All that matters, and figuring it out is a lifelong process. But I know that when and where you tell a joke can be as important as the joke itself. Comedians usually hate daytime gigs, especially outdoors. For some reason, it's just harder to make people laugh in the sunlight. Sometimes a joke works great with one crowd but dies with another. If I'm in Texas and I do a bit that pokes fun at kids with gluten allergies, the crowd loves it. If I do it in Portland, not so much.

Back around 2014, I was booked to perform at a marriage conference. I know what you're thinking: Why would anyone book me—a guy who at that point had not only never been married but struggled to maintain any sort of fruitful long-term relationship—at a marriage conference? The answer is, "I have no idea," but I was still a struggling stand-up back then, and I took whatever gigs I could get.

The guy who was speaking before me was giving a very earnest lecture about the massively popular couples-counseling book *The Five Love Languages*. If you don't know anything about it, the book basically says that everyone expresses and receives love in one of these languages: gifts, quality time, physical touch, words of affirmation, or acts of service. The key to a healthy relationship is understanding your partner's love language. (Hey, I just saved you $15.99, and two hundred pages of reading! You're welcome.) Anyway, I've always been pretty skeptical of those kinds of books, but the audience loved this guy's sermon. There were couples in the crowd who were crying and hugging for the first time in years. Marriages were being restored and renewed. After he finished, I went out and my first line was, "I think my love language is physical acts of quality touch." It did not land. Everyone was mortified. My entire set after that was pretty rickety.

I look back on it now, and there was nothing wrong with

that joke. I mean, it's a solid B-plus joke. But my timing was completely off. For starters, back then, nobody in the audience knew who I was and what my sense of humor was like. People had no frame of reference for me at all. If I had gone out there and done twenty or thirty minutes of material, let the crowd get to know me, gotten them on my side, and then dropped that joke, it would've delivered. But coming straight out of the gate with it, the audience just saw me as some punk kid who was making fun of something that was incredibly meaningful to them. So I learned my lesson, and you probably guessed it: I wasn't invited back.

TOO SOON?

During my Focus on the Family internship, I decided that I liked living in Colorado Springs a lot and wanted to stay there after the internship was finished. I had started attending New Life Church there, a massive evangelical congregation led by a pastor named Ted Haggard. Haggard was probably the most charismatic person I'd ever met. People were just drawn to him. When he was giving a sermon, people would be transfixed. The church seemed to be doing good work too. People were deepening their relationships with God and getting help in their marriages and with parenting. All the things that churches are supposed to be good at, this church was great at. But looking back on it now, Ted also talked a lot about homosexuality and how wrong it was.

If that name, *Ted Haggard,* rings any bells for you, you probably understand the subtext of all this. That November, the story broke that Haggard had been paying a male prostitute for sex and crystal meth. Haggard was a prominent figure in the evangelical movement, and the story was a huge national scandal.

Within the evangelical world, the sex and drugs were obviously a huge issue, but what made Haggard's downfall a big story outside church circles was the hypocrisy. Haggard had been decrying homosexuality. He was very public in supporting an amendment to the state constitution that outlawed same-sex marriage. In fact, that was the reason this male prostitute had come forward with the story in the first place. So for him to have been secretly doing all the things he was railing against was a big problem. He was fired from New Life but a few years later started up a new church across town.

I can look back now and see that the whole episode was filed pretty deeply into my subconscious, though one of the big lessons I took from it—that if you've got secrets, you better be sure to lock them down real tight—was almost certainly not the one I should have. It would take me a while and plenty of heartache to unlearn it.

There was another lesson for me too, though maybe one that was more on point. Everyone had loved Haggard and had invested so much of their faith in him, so when the scandal broke, it shook them to their core. He was hardly the first Christian leader to fall from grace so publicly (the sex scandals involving Jim Bakker and Jimmy Swaggart had been huge news in the eighties) and obviously wouldn't be the last. So why do we continually follow people instead of following God? Why do we expect humans to be anything but, well, human?

At the time, I dealt with whatever discomfort I might have had about Haggard the way I dealt with most things: I made it into a joke. At the Christmas party at church that year, I did a little comedy set and started it by apologizing for not being around the church more recently.

"I know you all haven't seen me around New Life lately," I said evenly. "That's because I've actually been going to Ted's." I let the silence hang in the air for a few seconds. I could hear some gasps. Then I broke the tension. "You know, Ted's . . . *Montana Grill*. They have a really nice brunch over there." It wasn't the most sophisticated joke, but it got a huge laugh.

Since Haggard left, he'd become *persona non grata* around New Life. His books were taken out of the church bookstore. His name was removed from literally everything on the church campus. He was not to be spoken of. So my mentioning him in a comedy set was saying the unsayable. And just like with the Andy Stanley joke, it was what people desperately wanted to hear, even if they didn't know it.

WANTS VERSUS NEEDS

In a way, stand-up comedy has always been a gift and a curse for me. Very early on in my comedy career, when I was just starting to kind of become a thing, I did a show at a church and afterward there was a long meet-and-greet line. I would typically say hi, have a quick photo taken, and make a joke about something. This one night, we were in Short Pump, Virginia. Yes, that is the name of the town. I remember a young girl and her mother coming through the line. The daughter had several casts on—at least two on each elbow—and braces on her legs. I chatted with her and asked her about her health. We snapped a photo, and I signed something for her. I didn't really think twice about it, until the next morning, when I got a Facebook message from her mom. She just wanted to thank me for the amazing show and taking the time to meet and talk to her daughter. She told me I was her daughter's favorite comedian and that she has a degenerative bone disease. She's typically wheelchair bound but wanted to stand to meet her favorite comedian. The line was long and the girl was starting to get weak, but she powered through, and after meeting me, she left smiling. It was the happiest she'd ever seen her daughter. Reading that made me cry. I printed out the message and kept it. I still have it and pull it out every once in a while when things aren't going so great for me.

Since that day, I've heard many stories like that. A woman going through a brutal divorce said she watched my comedy videos as an escape. A guy who was struggling with depression said my videos lifted his spirits. Someone once told me her parents are verbally abusive to each other in the house and whenever that happens she goes into her room, puts on her headphones, and watches my videos. That's heavy. I remember once before a show in Detroit at a church, the pastor pulled me aside. He said how grateful he was that I came to perform at their church and that there was someone who was going to commit suicide but decided to stay alive because she had something to look forward to: my show. Whoa. I was humbled by that, but as a comedian, I thought, *Good Lord, could you have at least waited until after the show to tell me that?* No pressure.

I don't say any of this to laud myself or to claim to be anything greater or better than I am. But for any human being, that is all a heavy responsibility to carry, and, frankly, one I was not—and am not—equipped to shoulder.

Bo Burnham, one of my favorite comedians, has a line in one of his parody songs that says, "Come watch the skinny kid with a steadily declining mental health / And laugh as he attempts to give you what he cannot give himself." If I had a mic, I would drop it. The best comedy makes you feel seen, feel heard, feel like you're part of something larger than yourself. I know that healthy people do not need to stand in front of a packed theater or watch view counts rise exponentially on one of their social media posts to feel that affirmation. But knowing that fact isn't enough.

Comedy isn't something I like; it's something I need. If that seems a bit melodramatic, well, yeah, sure it is. But sometimes I'm still that kid on the curb outside the tennis center waiting for his parents to pick him up or the guy who got turned down for prom or who didn't make the basketball team or whose bike got stolen or who got dumped by the first girl he loved. I could go on, but I'm sure you get the picture. What that guy wants, what he needs, is love, approval, likes, applause, laughs—and lots of them. So imagine what happens when that guy with that big gaping hole in his chest gets onstage, tells jokes, and finds something that can fill that hole, if only for a little while.

16

CANCEL JOHN CRIST!

In summer 2016, I had just started to headline at comedy clubs. That means I was the guy who performed last. My name was on the marquee. It's a big deal when comics make this transition from opener or middle act to headliner. One of my first headliner assignments was at the Loony Bin, a comedy club in Little Rock, Arkansas, and the guy who featured before me was a comic named Brett Eastburn. He was born with no arms and no legs, which honestly, in comedy, isn't that uncommon. Okay, I mean *that* is uncommon, but what I'm saying is for a comedian to have some sort of disability or abnormality isn't that uncommon. Josh Blue, who has cerebral palsy, is one of my favorite comics of all time and a guy I kind of came up with in Denver. He won *Last Comic Standing* in 2006. Drew Lynch has a speech impediment and was the runner-up on *America's Got Talent* in 2015. Because think about it: Comedy is a coping mechanism. Laughter is cathartic.

It was the same with Brett. He would make jokes about not having arms or legs, and people would double over laughing. Because we were both playing Wednesday night through Sunday night, the club put us up in a condo together, which is a pretty common arrangement. We ended up spending a ton of time together that week and really hitting it off. For comics, hitting it off means cracking on each other constantly. That's just the way it works.

The only problem that week was that Brett was impossible to follow onstage. He'd do a tight, funny set, get the audience laughing hysterically, then finish with this inspirational speech about how God put him on this planet for a reason and that if he can overcome his disabilities to pursue comedy, anybody can take life by the horns and make their dreams come true. The crowd would go nuts. He'd get a standing ovation (which, I thought, was offensive, by the way). When he'd finish, audience members would have tears streaming down their cheeks. How am I, an able-bodied comedian, supposed to go onstage after that?

So, Wednesday night, I struggled. Thursday night, same deal. I was frustrated. Finally, I came up with a plan. For the big sold-out Friday-night show, I decided to go out onstage with my arm tucked up my sleeve. I had this idea that if I came out onstage like that, the crowd would think it was hilarious. They, in fact, did not. The audience was horrified. Brett had just endeared himself to them, and there I was, looking like I was mocking him for not having arms. It was super-uncomfortable to be in that room, but I doubled down.

"I just want to thank everybody for coming out tonight," I told the audience. "Me and Brett have been on the road for a year together overcoming our disabilities. It just means so much to have your support."

Crickets. The audience is just staring at me in disbelief. I realize at that moment that I haven't thought this all the way through. I don't really have any jokes about having one arm. Where can I go from here? It's all incredibly uncomfortable. People are appalled. A few walk out. I decide to bail out of the bit. I pull my arm out and tell the crowd that I was only kidding. That makes it even worse. They think I was making fun of Brett. In fact, I was making fun of my own inability to follow him. They don't know that we're buddies, staying in the same condo together, ripping on each other all week. There is no way to get the audience back. It turns into one of the worst shows I've ever done. I completely bomb. I walk offstage to no applause, but when I get to the greenroom, I see Brett *dying* of laughter. He can legit barely breathe.

"Dude, I have been doing stand-up comedy for fifteen years, and that's the funniest thing I've ever seen in my life," he told me. He was the only person in that club who could've saved me that night. He could've come out and signaled to the audience that he was in on the joke, that he thought it was funny. He could've given them permission to laugh. But like any good comic, he much preferred to watch me eat it.

It takes some time and experience to learn how to work yourself out of tight spots onstage. I remember working the Denver Improv one night when I was just starting out. My set was going well. I was about fifteen minutes into it and getting huge laughs. Sold-out show. I was doing lots of crowd work, needling the people close to the stage, when I noticed three women sitting right up front. One of them wasn't even looking at me, so I zeroed in on her.

"Listen, if I'm going to talk to you, the least you could do is look me in the eye while I do it!" I told her confidently.

"She's blind," one of her friends replied.

"No way," I said.

With that, she unfolded her walking stick, the universal symbol of public blindness. I froze with horror and immediately began backpedaling as quickly as I could.

"I'm so sorry," I said. "I didn't mean to offend you. That was across the line. I'm a Christian. I never would have done that if I had known."

The crowd could see that I'd lost control, that I'd come out of character. The rest of the set tanked.

A few days after that, I was with Tim Hawkins and explained what had happened. I told him that I offended this woman, felt awful about it, and then really ate it onstage. I really respect Tim as a comic and look up to him for advice. He told me, "If you ever dig yourself a hole onstage, never back out. Never. The only way out is to keep digging."

"That sounds great in theory," I said, "but what would you have done in that scenario?"

"Easy," he told me. " 'You're blind and you're sitting in the front row of a comedy show? That's kind of a selfish move, don't you think?' "

He was right. That line would've really landed. It would've saved the show. As a matter of fact, after I bungled through the rest of that set in Denver, I'd asked the bartender to send the blind woman backstage so I could apologize to her again, in person. She came back to the greenroom with a giant smile plastered on her face. She wasn't upset at all. She told me she goes to the club every weekend because she loves to put comics in uncomfortable positions. That was her way of coping with her disability. She wants to laugh about it. She wants to feel like everyone else in the club. By getting all earnest about it, I'd really taken that opportunity away from her. She just wanted to be part of the fun.

SHOOT YOUR SHOT

I learned my lesson, though. A year or so later, I was playing Laffs Comedy Café in Tucson, Arizona, and down in front of the stage was a table of about ten guys who were all in their twenties. They were drunk and loud, and at some point, I asked them what they were all doing there. They told me they were on a bowling team. They liked to bowl and then go to the comedy club afterward. Fair enough. A few minutes later, one of them got up from the table on crutches and began to walk toward the bathroom.

"Hey, why is that guy on crutches?" I asked this table, assuming he'd gotten in a bar fight or drunkenly fallen off a curb or something silly like that.

One of the guys still seated shook his head. "Dude," he shouted, "he has cerebral palsy."

Yikes. Same feeling as with Brett and the blind woman. I could feel the air coming out of the room. I'd crossed a line. I'd gone too far. But I remembered what Tim had told me: Keep digging.

"Yeah? Who's the idiot captain of this bowling team that chose a dude with cerebral palsy to be on the team?" The club exploded with laughter. The guy on the crutches was laughing the hardest! I had the crowd back. No one was really offended. Everyone was still having a good time.

Look, comedy is not an exact science. Not everyone who is offended is wrong. There are times when I push into a sensitive area and miss the mark. There are times when I say things out of ignorance that I later realize are, well, ignorant. I remember doing a joke once about the tone of voice people read their texts in. One of the punch lines was about how the voice a guy was using to read a text from his wife made it sound like she was home alone with nasal congestion and Down syndrome. Not the best joke I've ever told, but also not the worst. After a show when I did that joke, a husband and wife waited at the back of a long line of people to talk to me. When everyone else had left and I was packing up my gear for the night, they approached me.

"We drove four hours to see your show tonight," the wife told me. "We love your comedy. We've seen all your videos. We think you're hilarious. We also have a daughter with Down syndrome. I don't think you understand that when you do that joke, for us, that joke just made us really sad."

I stood there and listened to these parents tell me about their daughter, how incredible she was, and also the unique challenges of her life, and I realized they were right. I genuinely appreciated that this couple took the time to talk to me about it. They didn't light me up on Twitter or call for my head on a stake. They didn't insist that everyone had to unfollow me and that bookers should cancel my dates. They told me their story, and I quickly could see that they were right and I was wrong. I'd made a mistake. I wanted to help, to lighten the load, to brighten people's days, and that joke didn't do that, so I never told it again.

WIDE OPEN (SAFE) SPACES

That's not the way these interactions usually go these days. Whenever someone makes a mistake, there is an immediate online outcry for the person to be fired, boycotted, excommunicated, burned at the stake, or somehow canceled. The idea that people screw up, learn from their screwups, and become better, more enlightened people has somehow been relegated to the dustbin of history.

This is especially bad for comedy. Just look what happened to Kevin Hart. He was slated to host the 2019 Oscars. Then someone went back through Hart's Twitter timeline and unearthed some homophobic tweets from 2009, as well as a routine he did onstage in 2010 in which he joked about trying to prevent his son from being gay. The pitchforks quickly came out for Hart. People were calling for a boycott of the Oscars. They were demanding he be fired from hosting them. There were calls for Nike and other brands to sever ties with him. Hart had already publicly walked back those tweets and jokes in 2014, but when he tried to tell people that he'd already addressed it, it only increased the outrage. So he apologized again and withdrew from hosting the Oscars. A month later, the public anger over Hart still hadn't subsided. He appeared on Ellen DeGeneres's daytime talk show and apologized again, and Ellen herself tried to convince him to retake his gig as host of the Oscars. He demurred. Over the course of the next month or two, he apologized again and again, on Twitter and in seemingly every interview he did, but the homophobia charges still hovered around him.

Most of the criticism of Hart was from so-called progressives. Despite the fact that Hart's views had clearly *progressed,* those people continually wanted to hold him accountable for the person he used to be. Isn't that the opposite of progress?

Whenever someone new arrives on our cultural radar—a debuting *Saturday Night Live* cast member, a freshly minted TikTok star, whoever—it is standard practice now to dig through that person's social media accounts in an attempt to ruin the best day of their life. We see it every year at the NBA draft. As these nineteen-year-old kids' dreams are coming true and their lives are being changed forever, an army of internet trolls looks to rain on their parade by dusting off some ill-advised tweet the kid sent when he was fourteen. Thank goodness cellphones with cameras and instant social media upload capabilities didn't really exist when I was in high school. Can you imagine the backlash I'd have gotten over the shaky footage of me elbow deep in a vat of Chick-fil-A lemonade?

We know now that social media companies reward these bouts of fake outrage. Their algorithms promote posts and comments that get the most responses. It doesn't matter if it's positive or negative—they just want lots of people clicking on it, commenting on it, and sharing it so they can sell those numbers to advertisers. If you post a comment underneath one of my videos saying that it's trash, that I'm a heretic and an unrepentant sinner, that is going to inspire responses. You are going to get that dopamine rush that comes with knowing that lots of people have feelings about your comment, and the social media company is going to make some money off those feelings.

I'm not saying that every person who is attacked by an internet mob deserves our sympathy. There are many bad people in the entertainment world who do genuinely bad things. They deserve to be held accountable. As do I. But this idea that everything that any of them has done in their artistic lives *must* be erased from history by the companies that did business with them is problematic. It takes agency away from all of us as consumers. If we're all genuinely upset by R. Kelly's behavior and we stop listening to his music, the market will take care of the rest. No doubt, my experience as being at the pointy end of that cancellation spear makes me pretty touchy about the issue overall and an imperfect vessel for this perspective. But it doesn't mean I'm wrong. (Or any wronger than I normally am about everything else.)

I understand the fears of the cancellation crusaders. People will still watch *Annie Hall* if we let them. They'll still listen to "Thriller." "I Believe I Can Fly" will still play behind inspirational video montages and in *Space Jam*. Mel Gibson's drunken anti-Semitic tirades haven't stopped TNT from rerunning *Lethal Weapon*. And why should it? That movie is great! I don't believe moonwalking to "Billie Jean" means that I am endorsing everything Michael Jackson ever did in his life. Aren't we sophisticated enough as humans to understand that great art is often made by very flawed artists?

It has been this way forever. Long before there was social media or the internet, there were artists behaving badly in their private lives. Picasso was an incorrigible misogynist, Gauguin impregnated a thirteen-year-old Polynesian girl, Caravaggio literally murdered someone over a tennis match (to be fair, I almost did the same in college), but discounting their art is the equivalent of discounting the theory of relativity because Einstein was a total jerk to his wife and kids. The work is the work. It's completely reasonable to view a piece of art—or any work—in the context of the artist's life, but if you can still enjoy *Rosemary's Baby* knowing what you know about Roman Polanski, no one should be able to stop you.

#CANCELJESUS

Right around the same time Kevin Hart was battling his cultural cancellation, a parallel story was developing in the world of Christian music. Well, parallel but opposite. Lauren Daigle, a massively popular contemporary Christian singer-songwriter, was under fire for appearing on Ellen's talk show and then later refusing to denounce homosexuality as a sin. As Hart was being lambasted for making intolerant comments about LGBTQ folks, Daigle was being lambasted for making tolerant ones. Christians were roasting her for it, saying she couldn't be a *real* Christian without unambiguously condemning homosexuality.

I spoke up for her, posting a somewhat rambling video to my Instagram, pointing out that she had done so much through her music, and basically told those who were questioning her faith that they should keep their opinions to themselves. I was just basically pointing out that Daigle, like the rest of us, is human. She has feelings, and these things people were saying about her were hurtful, and I didn't think she deserved that kind of treatment from an angry mob of people on the internet. I got crushed by the Christian media for that. "Christian Comedian John Crist Defends Lauren Daigle, Tells Critics to 'Just Shut Up'" blared one headline. Honestly, though, I stand by what I said.

I will also say this: Although Christian culture typically lags behind mainstream culture in most areas, we are totally out in front of the mainstream when it comes to this whole idea of canceling people. We were out there canceling folks long before it was cool. Just ask Galileo. *The Earth revolves around the sun? Sorry, dude, you're out.* And he's not the only one. There's been a long line of people since then who have been the focal points of intense scrutiny for not conforming to the religious cultural norms of the day.

I am confident that Jesus himself would struggle to avoid the judgmental *tsk-tsks* of Christianity's supposed army of online defenders. Long hair? Sandals? Hanging out with drunks, prostitutes, and sinners? If he were alive today, he'd be the first guy canceled. Oh wait, he already was.

Back around 2014, I did a show at a church in Duluth, Minnesota. At the time, I was kind of a one-man band, crisscrossing the country on my own to play gigs wherever I could find them. Those could be really lonely nights, and after finishing that Duluth gig, I fell almost immediately into a deep depression. I mean, let's be honest, it's Duluth: There's plenty to be depressed about, even more so when you decide that the best cure for your loneliness is to belly up to the bar at the Holiday Inn near the airport there. So, there I was at the bar, feeling sad, alone. To complete this portrait of desolation and desperation for you, I was also trying to text some woman I'd met to meet me for a drink. Oh, and she was married. I think that's important to mention just so you can see how dark things were for me in those days, how much I had lost my way. She never did come meet me, and it was a gloomy little scene that night.

A week or so later, I told a therapist about it all, and he asked me, "What do you think Jesus would think of you being there like that, in that bar texting that woman?"

I thought about it for a second. "Well, the Jesus I grew up

learning about would be ashamed of me, embarrassed for me. He'd probably walk by the bar on the way to preach or care for the sick and say something like, 'You just performed in a church, you call yourself a Christian, and you're here at a bar, trying to entice some married woman to meet up with you? Hypocrite. I'm embarrassed of you.'"

My therapist listened and then shook his head. "I bet if Jesus saw you there, he'd sit down right next to you. He'd say something like, 'You think I don't know what it feels like to be alone? All my closest friends left me to get crucified. I know loneliness. You think I don't know what it feels like to be sad? My friend Lazarus died. I know sadness. I am here with you.'"

I think too often we see Jesus as a superhero. Sure, he is God. He fed the poor; he healed the lame; he turned water into wine. But he was also a man. He knew sadness. He knew pain. Talking to that therapist was the first time I ever began to consider that Jesus might not be some distant authority figure keeping tally of everything I was doing wrong and that he might actually be on my side. But I wasn't sure if I was ready to believe it.

17

LIFE ON THE ROAD (TO RUIN)

Not too long ago, I boarded an airplane to fly from Nashville to Denver. It's a pretty long flight, so I was prepared: cellphone at 100 percent, Wi-Fi purchased, podcasts downloaded. You get it. Then this guy sat down in the seat next to me. He looked like a normal human being, but, trust me, he was not. He just sat down, and for the entire three-plus hours we were in the air and taxiing, he didn't take out a laptop, he didn't watch a movie, he didn't put in AirPods and listen to music, he didn't read a book or magazine, and he never once pulled out his phone. I was astounded and, frankly, a little horrified. *What is wrong with you, dude? What, are you just happy with your life? You are content to sit there for hours with nothing but your own thoughts keeping you company?*

Cellphones, in particular, have become an indispensable part of our daily lives, especially mine. For me, the diversion provided by our phones has become a necessary part of the social order. It's like the adult version of a pacifier. If I'm standing in line at the post office, I'm looking at my phone. If I'm in an elevator with you, you better take out your phone. Don't just stand there, blank faced, like a psychopath.

Our phones have become the ultimate social lubricants. Wherever you are, you can always avoid looking lonely—if maybe not actually cease *being* lonely—by scrolling through your phone. I mean, in the pre-cellphone era, what did people do when one person arrived at a restaurant five minutes before the other person? Just sit there quietly and wait? I was at dinner with a buddy recently, and he got up to go to the bathroom and left his phone on the table. WHAT? That is the whole reason you go to the bathroom. To. Check. Your. Phone. Staring at your phone has become a universally accepted way of signaling to the world that you are, in fact, a contributing member of society, that you have important people trying to reach you, important things going on in your life, something else that you are engaged in besides sitting on a park bench on a Wednesday morning.

NOTHING GOOD HAPPENS AFTER NOON

By 2014 or so, I was constantly driving alone from Denver to far-flung locales to play shady gigs that I'd often procured through even more shady bookers. I didn't care, though, because I was obsessed with comedy. I might drive fifteen hours for a one-hour show at a church in Tucson, Arizona, or at a half-empty bar in a derelict mining town in North Dakota. Then I'd park at a motel but sleep in my car because I wasn't getting paid enough for these shows to afford a room.

Back then, I thought a motel parking lot was the safest place to sleep. By comparison, a dark, empty lot outside, say, an office complex seemed dangerous, and I once got a lecture from a police officer for sleeping in my car on the side of the interstate. Apparently, the side of the highway is a good place to sleep only if you want to meet shady drifters or get plowed into by oncoming vehicles. Anyway, I'd bunk down in these hotel parking lots, pull out a pillow I'd brought with me for this occasion, and actually get a good night's sleep!

I got an agent who helped book college gigs, which could be a mixed bag, to say the least. They generally paid decent, but you never knew what the show was going to be like. I remember playing what comedians call a "nooner" at a college in northern Minnesota that has to rank among the worst gigs I've ever done. A nooner is an afternoon show, typically in a college food court, student-activities common area, or library. But at this point, I had just started traveling to do comedy, so I was actually really proud of this gig. I can remember bragging to all my comedy buddies about how I was leaving town for this Minnesota show. So I drove all the way to the college, got to the student center, and saw a microphone placed right in the middle of the common area. Taped to the microphone stand were my check and instructions for how to turn on the sound system. I was contracted to perform for an hour, starting at 1:30 P.M. There was no introduction, no emcee, no other person there besides me who really had any sense that a show was supposed to take place. So I followed my instructions, tapped the mic, and made an announcement.

"Hey, I'm John, and I'm a comedian, and I'm here to do a comedy show for you today!"

There were a dozen or so people scattered around the common area, studying, talking with friends. None seemed interested. I distinctly recall one kid looking up at me, then taking his headphones from around his neck and putting them on. It was a real power move on his part, and as demoralizing as I found it, I needed that check, and I was gonna complete that hour. It went down as probably one of the worst shows of my entire life. And what was worse, I couldn't just sleep this one off. It was midafternoon!

After the show, I was feeling kinda low, and this was in the years before I'd started drinking, so I fell back on my first vice, McDonald's drive-through, to cheer me up. I took it back to my room, because this time, payment for the gig actually included a motel room. (For the record, that's *motel* with an *m*, not *hotel* with an *h*. Small difference in spelling; *huge* difference in experience.) But when I got to the motel, the room didn't seem to have any functioning heat, and this was northern Minnesota, so it was freezing. But ever the resourceful traveler, I drew myself a hot bath, got in, and then ate my Big Mac and fries in the bathtub. That has to rank among the saddest moments of my life at the time.

But as bad as that day was, I was generally pretty happy back then. Bad gigs were quickly in the rearview mirror, and there were more shows to come. The next one was usually better, or at least I could convince myself it was going to be. I did almost everything myself in those days. I booked most of the gigs, I sent the contracts, I arranged my travel, I updated the website, I made sure I got paid, I dragged two big bags of merch to sell after the show, and I traveled alone. I wasn't making great money, but I kept my overhead low, and if everything went to plan, I could make enough to keep the machine going. But the margins were excruciatingly tight, and everything didn't always go to plan.

Once I could afford to fly between gigs, I'd generally try to book three shows every weekend. Those shows were often nowhere near each other. It was not unusual for me to do Thursday night in Seattle, Friday night in Indianapolis, and then Saturday night in Phoenix. If I missed a flight, that usually meant missing a show and losing out on the couple hundred bucks that I was counting on. It was unbelievably stressful, but I kept grinding. Part of it was surely an ambition to move up the comedy ladder, but another part of it was something a little more ineffable. I needed those shows to fill me up. I needed those laughs. I needed to get more social media followers so my Facebook and Instagram posts would get more likes, more comments, more affirmation for me. So, yeah, *totally* healthy.

It was becoming a vicious cycle, but from a career standpoint, it all seemed to be going in the right direction. The shows were getting bigger. There was a sense that things were starting to happen for me. I was like a high school basketball prospect who was about to pop, with college scouts lurking in the back rows of the gym bleachers, muttering things like, "This kid is gonna be special." Better opportunities seemed to be just around the next corner for me. I was auditioning for TV pilots. Important-seeming people wanted to have meetings with me.

In 2014, I moved to Los Angeles, to be closer to all this, but still spent most of my time on the road. People from back home were impressed that I was living in Hollywood. The reality was that I was living as the third person in a two-bedroom condo. I lived in the closet. Literally. Many of my shows were on the East Coast, so I was frequently waking up before 4 A.M. to catch a 6 A.M. cross-country flight to make it to a gig that night. Every weekend seemed to be a different insane route. Cleveland–Tampa–Austin. Charleston–Tulsa–St. Louis. Lexington–Providence–San Diego. Flight. Rental car. Fast food. Motel. Repeat.

It was a lot. Some of my close friends and family started to voice a little concern. A few suggested that maybe I needed to take some time off. I was like, *To do what?* They didn't get it. Out on the road, I was a god. (Lowercase *g,* though.) Everyone loved me. They were excited that I'd come to their town. They'd watched all my videos. They couldn't wait to meet me. I was starting to have meet and greets with lines of people who wanted to take a photo with me or buy a T-shirt from me. If I was to take some time off, all I had waiting for me back in L.A. was a sad-looking reality that looked like every other sad-looking reality everywhere else. There was trash that needed to be taken out and mail that needed to be picked up. Who wants to be that average nobody when you can be out there on the road feeling like the center of the universe? So I kept going. The affirmation machine needed fuel.

ON THE RUN

In late February 2016, I was scheduled for a weekend that was fairly typical: Friday night at Woods Church, a big congregation in Warren, a suburb of Detroit; Saturday at Paul Smith's College, a small liberal arts college three hours north of Albany in the Adirondacks; and Sunday at the Comedy Works in Denver. That meant a 3:30 A.M. wake-up call for a 6:00 A.M. crosscountry flight, layover in Chicago (because I couldn't afford to fly direct), baggage claim, two suitcases, rental-car shuttle, rush-hour traffic, all to get to the venue at about 5:00 P.M. Then one hour of merch setup and sound check before doors opened. Again, all fairly typical.

I arrived at the church in Warren, got all my gear set up, met the pastor, and did the show, which went fine. A few thousand people. Standing ovation. A cousin of mine was there and brought her kids, who were big fans. I should've been on top of the world, but instead I left there with a sense that something wasn't quite right and hadn't been for a while.

I drove to a gas station and bought a six-pack of beer. Once I'd moved to L.A., slowly I started drinking more and more. That particular night, I felt as if I needed something to take the edge off, which, I'm sure, is a sign that all is not entirely well. I remember walking out of that gas station and looking carefully to make sure nobody who was at that church show happened to see me. It wasn't like I was scoring heroin or anything, but even just a six-pack of beer would create some unwelcome whispers in church circles.

That night, I went back to my motel and figured I'd have a few beers and do what I normally did those evenings: toggle between my various social media accounts and soak up the love. It usually would flood in. *John's amazing. His videos are great. His stand-up is even better. He's good looking too.* Maybe I could also find a fan to flirt with and exchange some Snapchat photos with until I fell asleep. Especially on a night like that one, when I was feeling lonely, depressed, somehow unfulfilled, the internet would always set me right. It wasn't quite the same adrenaline rush as being onstage, but it was the next best thing, a fix to tide me over until my next show.

So, there I was, drinking alone at a Days Inn in a dreary Detroit suburb, looking at my phone, when suddenly it went dead. That little Apple logo showed up on the screen, and then the phone died completely.

It all just stopped.

I fiddled with the phone a little but couldn't get it to start back up. Figuring that something was wonky with the battery, I plugged it in, put my head down on the pillow for a minute, and instantly fell asleep. Or passed out. Maybe a combination of the two. I'm not sure.

My phone was still dead the next morning, and without it to wake me up, I overslept and missed my 6:00 A.M. flight to Albany. I had my laptop, so I checked for other flights, but there was nothing that would get me to Albany in time to make my next show, and it was all too expensive anyway. I really couldn't cancel the show—I wanted the money, but probably more important, I needed that rush. I got on MapQuest and saw that it was about an eleven-hour drive. Even though I couldn't drive through Canada, because I didn't have my passport, if I left right away, I could make it to Paul Smith's College in time for the show.

I was helpless without my phone. I wrote down the directions from MapQuest on the back of an envelope, like some sort of Neanderthal, but I didn't even make it out of the Days Inn parking lot before I was stumped. *North on Route 53. Is that right or left? How am I supposed to know which way is north? Am I supposed to navigate by the stars? Did I need a compass?* I made it about six miles before I had to pull over at a McDonald's, take out my computer, and connect to the Wi-Fi to recheck the directions.

My problems didn't go away once I finally got myself headed the right way. Normally, if I had eleven hours to myself on the road, I'd spend most of it, in some way, on my phone. I'd be checking my social media; I'd be playing music or a podcast through it; I'd be texting and talking with friends. (That near-fatal car wreck I told you about at the beginning of the book had somehow not really soured me on texting and driving.) And there seemed to be nothing on the radio either. It felt like no escape: eleven hours, nothing to keep me company but my own thoughts. And there were a lot of them. All my deepest issues—my worries about my career, my romantic failures, my doubts about my faith, my longing for my parents' attention and approval, the rising fear that I couldn't live up to the clean-cut image I was creating for myself—had been silenced for so long by my obsession with comedy and social media. Now with no phone to distract me, it all seemed to come rushing down on top of me. I felt alone. Very alone.

I tried to outrun it. Like, literally. I was driving this blue Ford Focus like a madman—not only because I needed to get to this next gig in time but because the voices in my head were so loud that I couldn't stand to be locked in the car with them. My loneliness was coalescing into rage, mostly at myself, and it was boiling up inside me: *What am I doing out here? This is stupid. I don't need this. But at the same time, I DO need this—desperately.* I kept driving, faster and faster.

I wasn't out of Michigan before I got my first speeding ticket. *So what?* I thought. *Once I make it to the show, I'll have enough money to pay ten speeding tickets.*

An hour later, another set of flashing blue lights. A second speeding ticket. Calloused and unmoved, I took the ticket and added it to the one I already had.

And then . . . a third ticket.

A fourth ticket.

I couldn't connect. I felt numb. I didn't care. I wouldn't say I was suicidal, but I wasn't that far from it either. I *wanted* to go to jail. If I got arrested, then I could tell everyone, "Sorry, I can't do this anymore. I need help." For so long, my phone had been my pacifier, keeping me docile and unreflective. It had been silencing my demons. Now they were unleashed. And they were screaming.

Miraculously, somehow I made it to the college without killing anyone, including myself. The campus was kind of in the middle of nowhere, and it had just started snowing as I pulled in there around 5:30 P.M. The show was in the food court, and let me tell you right now, it was horrible. There were ten people there—I know, because I counted and wrote the number down. At one point, I had to pause a joke because someone pressed the ice maker and I couldn't talk over it, even with a microphone.

The show ended around 9:00 P.M., and it had been dumping snow outside the entire time I was there. There was about a foot accumulation on the ground, and it continued to snow. My rental car was basically buried. I hadn't yet booked a hotel for that night because I normally booked one on Priceline using my phone, and it was still dead. As I packed up my stuff from the show, it occurred to me that I had no place to go. I looked and the only person left in the building was this pimply-faced, nineteen-year-old student-activities director. I asked him if I could just sleep on the couch there in the student center. He looked at me like I was crazy. Which, I suppose, I was.

"Uh, no, you can't do that. I've got to lock it up. You can't stay here."

"I don't know if I can drive in this," I told him.

"Yeah," he agreed. "It doesn't look safe at all."

"Are there any hotels right around here?"

He shook his head. "No, the closest place is a ski lodge that's about twenty miles away."

I started to cry. I really had no idea what to do, and pinning my hopes on this student-activities director was clearly a losing cause. I walked out of the student center with him, and he locked the door and continued toward his dorm, leaving me alone in the snowy parking lot. I dragged my bag of merch to the car—which was really heavy because I'd sold exactly none of it, by the way—tossed it in, and decided my only real option was to try to drive through the snow and get to that lodge. The kid had given me vague directions, so I slowly made my way. It was dark, I was fighting back tears, the roads were covered with a foot of snow, and it was still blizzard conditions. I remember thinking, *If this car goes off the road, it's over for me, and I'm okay with that.* I'd never felt so low, so inconsequential, before. I didn't want to die, but I didn't want to live.

I pressed on, driving into the night on a two-lane winding road. I couldn't see more than twenty feet in front of me. And remember, no phone, which means no calling anyone if anything happened, and, perhaps more important, no GPS. Everything depended on that kid's directions.

Believe it or not, I found the lodge. My first thought upon seeing it was, *Is this place even open?* If you're picturing the Overlook Hotel from *The Shining,* well, this place wasn't nearly that nice. It was small and old with lots of dark wood paneling. I'm pretty sure that on the outside, it just said "Hotel." It was more like a hunting lodge, where you could get in from the cold, take a hot shower, and stay warm for the night, all of which sounded fine to me at that moment. Fortunately, they had rooms available, though I would've happily slept on the couch in their lobby if they would've let me. Still phone-less and still needing to be up at 4:30 A.M. to get to the airport for my next flight and next show, I gave the guy at the desk twenty bucks to bang on my door and wake me up early the next morning. Especially with how depressed and sad I was, I'm still pretty proud of the ingenuity it took to pull that off.

When the morning came, it had stopped snowing, but I was feeling no better. I still had to make it to the Albany airport by 8:00 A.M. so I could catch my flight to Denver. I was blitzing down the interstate, when I got pulled over yet again. I eased my car to the side of the road, then rolled down the window as the cop approached.

"Sir, do you know how fast you were going?"

I didn't. And I didn't care. I was just exhausted.

"License and registration, please."

I rifled through the glove box and then handed them over.

"Maybe you thought I was going to have pity on you and let you out of this ticket," he told me, "but you were going eighty in a fifty-five."

None of it mattered. He gave me the ticket, and I stayed there at the side of the road. I finally broke. The tears flowed. The tears kept flowing. But this was a good thing. I felt emotions. I could express them. When I finally got to the airport in Albany, I called my parents from a pay phone with tears in my eyes and told them I was coming home. I needed a break.

Incidentally, though, before I went home to my parents, I actually did make my flight to Denver and fulfilled that final commitment at the Comedy Works. It was one of the best shows of my entire life. Being on the road for so long, I'd been on auto-pilot in my act, but now it was all loose and freewheeling. I felt reconnected to my jokes, to the audience, maybe even to my-self. I killed onstage that night. Everything in my life seemed to be falling apart, but the stand-up was still there for me. Sure, there were bad shows here and there, but comedy could come through big. However, I knew I needed a break.

The next day, I flew home to my parents' house in Georgia. I canceled all my stand-up dates for the near future and got off social media. Well, I mean, technically I didn't get off social media. I literally didn't have a cellphone. And for the first time ever, I didn't want one.

18

KNOCK, KNOCK. WHO'S THERE?

In fall 2018, I got a tour bus for the first time. A lot of stories of poor life choices have started with a sentence like that one. The bus was like a physical manifestation of the fact that I wasn't just some struggling comic anymore. I'd been used to traveling alone or maybe with one or two others, but now I had a bus full of people—managers, merch sellers, support comics—and they all worked for me. It was a thirteen-week tour, which is a looong time to be living in a three-hundred-square-foot capsule with twelve other people.

The tour was amazing: packed theaters, meet and greets, standing ovations. I felt like I'd spent years on the road honing my craft, and people were finally appreciating it. I remember one show where the greenroom had windows overlooking the parking lot. As we did the sound check, I could see the line of people gathering and growing. It was a hundred yards long, then two hundred yards, and then it wrapped around the building. You'd think that would be a cool moment for me to witness, but it made me very uncomfortable. It was strange to see how much these people liked me, when, truly, at that moment in time, I didn't really feel the same way about myself.

On that tour, I met people who watched my stand-up while they were getting chemotherapy. I visited a children's hospital where a huge fan of mine was fighting for his life. Of course, that stuff is inspiring, but it also felt darkly ironic: I was a guy trying to fight for my own life and well-being with varying degrees of success on any given day, and here were all these other people looking to me to do the same for them. Remember that Bo Burnham lyric "Come watch the skinny kid with a steadily declining mental health / And laugh as he attempts to give you what he cannot give himself"? It was *that*.

The idea of someone driving eight hours to see me makes me squirm. When someone tells me I changed their life, I want to hide in a closet. It's a great paradox that we all deal with on some level: I want everyone to look at me and love me, but I don't think I'm worth being looked at or loved. *What happens when these people I've supposedly inspired learn about the real, flawed me? Well, the intro video is playing, so let's push those emotions down and go tell some fart jokes!*

My issues on that tour weren't the shows themselves. It's the comedian's curse: The shakier my emotional state got, the better shows seemed to go. It was the twenty-three other hours in each day that were the problem.

The whole atmosphere felt claustrophobic. And lonely. It began to feel a lot like that car ride from Detroit to upstate New York a few years before. Yeah, this time there were distractions—my phone, people on the bus—but it wasn't enough to quiet all those same questions that had never really been answered: *What am I doing out here? What am I trying to prove? Who is this guy these people wanted to see onstage every night? What do I have to offer them? What really happened in that final episode of* Breaking Bad?

The lines I'd once drawn in my personal life, which had been guided by my faith, got blurrier. I was drinking more. I felt trapped on that bus. My entire day was scheduled. It belonged to someone else: sound check, press, photo shoot, show, meet and greet, repeat. I know for many that sounds like a dream, but I could feel myself unraveling. There's an ancient Chinese curse—or more likely, just something a lot of non-Chinese people like to cite as an ancient Chinese curse—that says "May all your wishes come true." That was me. I had everything I'd ever wanted and I'd never been so miserable in my life.

I guess that's why when I'd finally get some "me time," I'd go all out. On days off back home, I'd drink heavily and either go out to bars and clubs or have women spend the night at my house. On the road, I'd sometimes have women meet me in my hotel room. I just didn't want to be left alone with my thoughts.

It wasn't really the physical gratification I was after; it was attention and affirmation. I could probably trace this back to the girls in high school who didn't want to date me, the one who rejected me for prom, getting dumped by my first girlfriend—or even further, to just feeling overlooked as a kid—but nailing down the origins of this problem is probably less important than just acknowledging it exists.

Regardless, after some woman would post something like, "I love John. His show was amazing!" sometimes I'd DM her. If the chat got flirty, I'd steer it into increasingly sexual directions. The woman might tell me she had a boyfriend or a husband, but

I didn't care. I was desperate for more affirmations, more fuel, more opportunities to fill that emptiness deep inside me.

I remember performing at a church, then slipping a woman my hotel-room key at the meet and greet so nobody would see us leave together. If you're thinking, *This guy is a touring comedian. He's not married. Isn't this normal behavior?* you'd be right. But everyone knew me as this buttoned-up Christian guy. I wasn't the person I played onstage, and that was a problem I didn't really want to face.

LOCK ME UP

Life went on like that for a while. I'd go on Christian tours and perform at churches, all the while having this private life going the opposite direction. But my career was on a rocket ship. At one point, I was vacationing with my girlfriend in St. Lucia (a flex), sitting on the deck of our villa (another flex), when I got a call from my agent. He'd promised not to call while I was vacationing, so I figured it must be important.

"Welcome to the club, John," he told me. "You just got your first Netflix special!"

I was so happy that I cried. For a brief moment, I felt accepted. In 2019, a Netflix special was the pinnacle achievement for a stand-up, a sign you'd made it. And I had. I went back inside and had a glass of champagne with my girlfriend. Of course, I'd booked a villa out of sight from the rest of the hotel guests so they wouldn't see that she and I shared the same room.

That relationship ended late summer of 2019 because, well, of course it did. (Have you been paying attention to this book at all?) Shortly after, I was on tour in Minnesota and agreed to do a show at a maximum-security prison. This type of thing isn't as uncommon as you might think, though it was new for me. When I arrived, they gave me a tour. Even though it didn't look exactly like the *Shawshank Redemption*–style lockup of my imagination, it was still pretty grim: rows and rows of cells and a prison yard with brawny tattooed dudes lifting weights and playing basketball.

The prisoner giving us the tour was a seemingly sweet guy who matter-of-factly volunteered that he'd murdered someone a decade earlier. He introduced me to other inmates, and each would recite their name and what they were in for. "I'm Mike. I'm doing ten years for armed robbery." "Jake, kidnapping and felony assault." I was struck by the way they'd rattle off their crimes the way you might list your hometown or your favorite color. What they did was out in the open, and now they were being punished for it. They seemed remarkably at peace.

Looking around the prison at men lifting weights, playing cards, and whatnot, my overwhelming emotion was a strange one: jealousy. No joke. We're taught prison is the last place anyone wants to land, but for me, at that moment, the idea of not having to hide from my growing shame, not having to live in fear of the world discovering who I really am, to have all my sins out there, was incredibly appealing. Physically, these men were imprisoned, but mentally, they were free. I felt the opposite.

A week or so later, I had a show in Texas. Afterward, it was meet and greet, then hotel. Nights on the tour bus with my friends and tour-mates around were bearable, but nights alone in a hotel could be really rough. That hotel-room door closing *felt* like a prison-cell door slamming shut. With this thought looming, I did a few shots of tequila before the meet and greet, then popped in a piece of gum so nobody could smell the alcohol on my breath. Before heading to the hotel, I packed my backpack with three White Claws just so I could survive the night. Someone from the show agreed to meet me in my room, but by the time she arrived, I'd been drinking for a few hours already and passed out before anything very physical happened between us. That was beside the point for me anyway. I'd played four sold-out shows that weekend and lapped up the standing ovations, so there was no way I could simply go back to my hotel room by myself and watch *SportsCenter*. I couldn't handle that comedown. I needed alcohol to numb me and a woman to make me feel loved.

The next morning, I felt awful. Like soul-crushingly awful. Many of you have probably had hangovers that made you feel as though you needed to reevaluate your life. This wasn't that. This was deeper and more troubling. I went to the airport, slept through the first leg of my flight, then walked out into the terminal at Dallas/Fort Worth, where I had to change planes, feeling a profound sadness not unlike what I'd felt driving through the snowstorm in upstate New York years earlier. Looking back, it wasn't my actual behavior bringing up these feelings; it was the shame. Shame that I wasn't the guy people thought I was. Shame that I couldn't behave better. Shame that I had this secret life nobody knew about. I couldn't shake it. I walked into an airport bar and ordered a double shot of Tito's . . . at 9:00 A.M. It was the first time in my life I drank in the morning. My life was seriously out of whack, and I couldn't figure out how to fix it.

▨ NOVEMBER 7, 2019

There was a solution—not one I'd have ever proposed, but a solution, nonetheless. I was golfing one day back in Nashville, when my manager texted me that we needed to talk. He was coming over.

It was odd for my manager to insist on coming to my house. When I walked in and saw him and my sister Emma, who was working for me at the time, sitting in my living room, I kind of knew what this was about. He spilled out the details while my sister sat there in tears: A Christian website had been investigating me for six months. The publication was getting ready to publish an exposé on all the stuff I'd been hiding for years: the hookups, the sexting, the drinking. Some things in the article were true. Some weren't. But it didn't much matter at this point. It was all going to come out. If shame had a Super Bowl, this would be it: religion, sex, and fame. The publication had asked if I had a statement I'd like to make.

There's a scene at the end of one of my favorite movies, *The Fugitive,* where Tommy Lee Jones finally catches up with Harrison Ford. At that point, Harrison Ford is exhausted, tired of running, physically, mentally, emotionally. Tommy Lee Jones sees him and says, "It's over . . . It's over." Well, I remember collapsing into a recliner in my living room and thinking the same thing: *It's over.* The hiding, the running, the shame—it was all over. I knew there would probably be serious consequences for all this, but I didn't care anymore. I was relieved. I didn't know what the path forward was, but I hated my current situation.

The news story was set to post online at ten the next morning. I sent the magazine a statement and took responsibility for my actions. I was publicly professing to be a Christian, earning a living in Christian circles, yet behaving like a member of an eighties rock band on the road (minus the drugs and the mullet). Any criticism heading my way was fully earned.

I had a show scheduled for the night before the article was set to drop. Also, I was rehearsing my set for *The Late Late Show with James Corden,* which I was scheduled to appear on the following week. That was a big deal: Not only would it be my first time performing on late night, but it was to promote my forthcoming Netflix special. With all this going on, you can probably guess how the show went: I CRUSHED. Much like it had always been, the stage was a refuge from the pain of real life. To hear people laughing at my jokes filled me up, told me I was good enough, and made me forget, at least for a moment, that the rest of my world was in shambles.

The high didn't last. That night, I couldn't sleep. I just lay there in bed, playing out my future in my head, feeling sorry for myself. I tried to imagine what I was going to do with the rest of my life. Every possible situation quickly went to the worst-case scenario.

The next morning, ten o'clock came and went without the story being posted. For a brief moment, I wondered if maybe I'd been granted a reprieve. I went on a walk. Eleven o'clock, nothing. Noon, nothing. Maybe they'd read my statement of contrition and decided against publishing this exposé. For a moment, I was happy. Then I allowed myself to live in that reality for a minute, imagined my life returning to what it'd been the past few years: the secrets, the shame, the hiding, the loneliness, the anxiety over getting caught. I thought about the promise of freedom at that prison in Minnesota. I realized I didn't want to maintain the facade. I remember thinking, *If they don't publish the story, I will.*

As it turned out, they published it. The story itself was kind of underwhelming. As eighties rock stars go, I was definitely more Richard Marx than Nikki Sixx. My debauchery was distinctly minor league. But the story went into detail about a few women I'd been with, the sexting with married women, and something about me trading Winter Jam tickets for sexual favors, which wasn't true but was kind of funny since Winter Jam tickets were all of ten bucks. Not every detail in the story was accurate, but the overall gist was that I was a dirtbag and, worse than that, a gigantic hypocrite.

Do you know who the first people were at my doorstep once this all went down? My parents. Part of me didn't want them to come. My dad wasn't just a pastor; he was now the mayor of my hometown. I knew my parents would be mortified. I thought back to all the rules we had growing up, the emphasis on keeping up appearances, the paddle I'd faced after running on the roof of the church. But they didn't show up yelling. There was no judgment, no condemnation. (And thankfully, no paddle.) They dropped everything and just came and sat with me. For all the stories I've told about them previously in this book that maybe haven't portrayed them in the best light, this story right here is who they truly are. They were there for me on the darkest day of my life.

Of course, it felt indescribably awful to have all my worst traits on display for the world to see, but there was also a weird sense of liberation. With everything I feared coming true, my anxiety dissipated. That night, I slept like a baby. It reminded me of a line from *The Usual Suspects.* Chazz Palminteri's police detective character says, "Let's say you arrest three guys for the same killing. You put them all in jail overnight. The next morning, whoever's sleeping is your man. You see, if you're guilty, you know you're caught, you get some rest, you let your guard down." That was me.

My manager asked me if I wanted to tour that weekend. In my head, I was thinking, *Tour? Are you kidding? I'm never leaving my house again!* We canceled the rest of my tour.

That cancellation set off a firestorm. What was once nothing more than a Christian tabloid article with a bunch of "he said" / "she said" sources became bigger news. CNN, Fox News, and *USA Today* all picked up the story. It was everywhere. Netflix put my special on hold. *The Late Late Show* canceled my appearance. This all happened in a matter of hours.

Even though this was shaping up to be perhaps the first sex scandal in history where no one was having actual sex, I could tell it was going to be a sordid scene in Nashville for a while. It was a lead story on the local news, and I felt under siege. My therapist suggested I go to a rehab center in Arizona. That sounded fine. I wasn't sure I was addicted to anything, but rehab was preferable to sitting around my house alone, staring at my phone as the world seemed to be coming for my head. I would've agreed to sit with a polar bear on an arctic ice floe at that point if I could be promised that news cameras and all my problems wouldn't follow me there.

19

DESERT STORM

I arrived at the Meadows, a rehab facility in Wickenburg, Arizona, and, no joke, it felt like prison. I immediately had to surrender my phone and laptop. They took away my shoelaces and belt, standard operating procedure, so people can't hang themselves. That's how serious this place is. They even confiscated my hair gel because it was alcohol based. That bordered on cruel and unusual punishment. I need hair product. Food, water, shelter, and Paul Mitchell. That gel was the only thing standing between me and the abyss. Without it, I decided to do the only thing I could: I shaved my head.

Then it *really* felt like prison.

The Meadows is a world-renowned addiction-recovery center. Much later, when I told people I went to rehab, the first reaction was often, "For what? I read the story. Isn't that just being a single dude in your thirties?" I suppose there's a nugget of truth in that, but my main problem wasn't the things I'd been doing—though certainly acting like a self-centered jerk and treating women like they were disposable are problems. The real issue was how I'd been feeling about what I was doing.

I was consumed by shame. I couldn't stand to look at myself in the mirror.

Think about it like this: If you have a couple of beers with dinner and drive home, that might not be the best decision, but you're probably not going to be overcome with crippling shame because of your behavior. But let's say on that drive home, you get pulled over, blow into a Breathalyzer, get handcuffed and thrown into the back of the cop car and fingerprinted, have your mugshot taken, and spend a night in jail. That DUI is the public outing of your behavior. You're now a criminal. Your mugshot is in an internet database. You've been publicly outed as an idiot. The exposure—not the behavior—brings the shame.

THE BOOK OF JOB

Nobody knew who I was in rehab. For confidentiality, we all just went by our first names and the first initial of our last names, but nobody really cared who I was anyway. Nobody was interested in how many views my videos got or how many tickets I sold. The unhealthy John was dying without the recognition, but a new John was slowly being birthed.

I'd tried to deal with some of my issues before, but obviously it hadn't worked. The way I thought about sex and relationships with women was clearly unhealthy. I can't speak for all religions, but in my case, growing up, the solutions usually offered for these types of issues were to pray more, go to church more, and maybe get an internet filter so I wouldn't look at porn. I remember once being advised to wear a rubber band on my wrist and snap it every time I looked at a woman with lust. So, essentially, I was being taught to associate one of man's most primal instincts with pain and shame.

None of that dealt with the real underlying problems. I'd follow the church's ideas of therapy, and for a short while, shame and fear might cause me to look at less porn or drink less or not DM random women, but it didn't keep me from desperately *wanting* to do those things. The church's solution seemed to be to white-knuckle it. Remember that crazy drive from Detroit to upstate New York when I got five speeding tickets, then nearly drove off the road in a blizzard? That's what white-knuckling it looks like. All the religion that had been stacked on me in my life had played a big part in twisting me into the knots I was in, so looking to religion to untangle those knots didn't make much sense.

My first night in Wickenburg, I was told to write a letter to God. I couldn't stand the thought. I actually constructed mine more as a letter *from* God about his boy John Crist and his plans to screw up poor John's life. It was sarcastic, bitter, and filled with self-pity. Also, in retrospect, maybe a little bit funny.

"I'm gonna have him born to a huge family of eight kids," I wrote, ever so humbly taking on the voice of God. "He's going to get neglected and lost and bullied. I'm also going to make sure he gets turned down by lots of women when he's young. Turned down for prom and frat parties and stuff, so he's gonna have a HUGE hole in his soul. So the guy who got ignored by girls growing up—now I'm gonna give it ALL to him. THEN I'm gonna send him out on the road . . . alone for eight years. And I'm gonna give him a drinking problem and money to add to it." I closed the letter with God reveling in what was then my current situation: "I took his job, his dignity, literally everything from him. I sent him to the desert. Just like in the movies. Sent him to the desert to die. The end."

So, there I was, in the desert, wailing at God for what *he'd* done to *me,* ready to pack it in. I thought I was living out the book of Job, getting all "Why hast thou forsaken me?" at God for the plagues he'd visited upon me by making me a successful comedian. Yes, I know, I sound ridiculous, but, hey, it was day one of rehab. I hadn't learned anything yet!

Look, the church shaped who I am—mostly for better, but occasionally for worse. I'd always associated sex with shame. It was the thing we Christians didn't really discuss. Sex was reserved for marriage. Anywhere else, it was forbidden and dirty. So where does that leave me, a single guy in his thirties, getting a lot of attention for the first time in his life, with a healthy yearning for love and intimacy but slowly becoming resigned that all I'll ever really find are unhealthy versions of it? I felt surrounded by temptation but believed that giving in to it was a grave sin that would endanger my immortal soul. And I was afraid to talk about it with anyone who could really help because doing so might also sink my career. Hindsight is always twenty-twenty, so I can definitely see it all a little more clearly now.

THE HARD-KNOCK LIFE

Life wasn't easy at the Meadows. We'd wake up every day at 5:20 A.M., while it was still dark. Then there would be some of the things you might expect: meditation, yoga, therapy sessions, lectures, group counseling. Some days we'd have tai chi, equine therapy, or acupuncture. A month or so later, I was talking to my best friend, Isaac, and his wife and complaining about how tough it was. "We had to wake up so early, then meditate and do yoga before breakfast."

His wife, Katie, grabbed the phone. "John, I'm going to stop you right there. We have three kids under five! This place sounds incredible."

"You don't understand," I said. "I had to talk to therapists all day."

"Oh, you talked to actual adults all day? Your conversations weren't about *PAW Patrol* or wanting more Oreos? That sounds amazing!"

"I had to be drug tested every day! They watch you pee."

"Only one person watched you pee? That sounds like luxury to me!"

"No, it was a nightmare. There was no sexual activity whatsoever."

"This place sounds like a dream!"

In all seriousness, the therapy was helpful. In daily sessions, I unpacked the messier parts of my childhood. At one point, we were asked to role-play and relive a childhood trauma. I detailed a vacation I took with my extended family to an amusement park when I was ten. At these family gatherings, I always wanted to hang with my older brothers and cousins. I hated being shuffled off with the *little* kids. I wanted to be included. So when the older crew was going on the bumper boats, I begged my parents to let me go. They relented.

Everything was fine until my boat got bumped under a waterfall. My steering wheel got jacked all the way to the left, so I was just spinning in circles underneath this waterfall, getting soaked. I turned the wheel the other way but only succeeded in changing the rotation of the boat. Now I was spinning to the right, basically being waterboarded under this waterfall. But what really left a mark was that there I was, ten years old, spinning underneath the falls, panicked, screaming, crying, surrounded by my parents, my siblings, all the people in the world who were supposed to be looking out for me, and no one noticed a thing. Not a thing. I remember reliving this at the Meadows and thinking, *Mom, where are you? Dad, don't you see me here, nearly drowning? Is anyone going to help me? Anyone?*

I realized, as an adult, I was still that kid in the bumper boats, spinning out, overlooked, hoping to God someone would notice. So, of course, I'm desperate for attention, for love. So, of course, I became a comedian. With what other job can you go out every night and have thousands of people see you, hear you, and tell you that you're worth something?

It wasn't the schedule or the activities that made life hard at the Meadows. It was being cut off from the things that had sustained me for so long. Any lifeline to any type of dopamine rush was taken away. We couldn't do *anything*. No pleasure of any kind. Major addictions like drugs, alcohol, and sex were, of course, forbidden. But even lesser addictions were off limits. Cellphones, gone. Computers, gone. Television, gone. Music, gone. Fiction books, gone. Caffeine, gone. If you were one of those people who could get a runner's high, they'd limit you to fifteen minutes of exercise a day. It was nuts. But they wanted you to feel—maybe for some of us, for the first time in our lives—to really *feel*.

You also weren't allowed to do your job there. If you were a lawyer, you couldn't give legal advice. If you were a doctor, you couldn't diagnose people's medical issues. One guy was a male model: They made him pick all his clothes from the lost and found so he would look raggedy. As a comedian, I wasn't allowed to tell jokes. Really. I had to sign a humor contract promising I wouldn't try to make people laugh. The idea was to break us down and show us that we're not what we do. But after a lifetime of cracking jokes to put people at ease, now I had to sit in that tension all the time, which made me super uncomfortable.

The sadness could be really heavy in that place. One day in rehab, I was feeling incredibly low, and my therapist asked me what I wanted to do. I said, "Honestly, I want to get my cellphone back. I want to fly to Nashville, withdraw all my money out of the bank, go downtown, get drunk, meet women, and bring them back to my condo. I want to do that every night until I run out of money. And then I want to kill myself." That's what I legit told my therapist, because with the tools I had, that was the only solution I could think of, the only place for a short respite from the pain.

YOU'VE GOT MAIL

The first two weeks in Wickenburg, you were cut off from the outside world. No messages, no calls, nothing. Total communication blackout. During this time, a therapist asked me if I'd be open to having my parents visit for Family Week a few weeks later. I didn't want to make my parents drop whatever they were doing, fly across the country, and stay a week at a Days Inn all to be part of my rehab process. It was nice that they'd come to Nashville, but this was embarrassing. They don't want that. Let me just sit here out in the desert and be sad by myself. The therapist suggested that I keep an open mind about it and "trust the process," which is a thing people say a lot in rehab. Whatever.

After two weeks at the Meadows, the communication blackout was lifted. One morning, my name appeared on the whiteboard. That meant there was a message or mail for me. It was the first time my name had been on that board. It was a glimpse back into the outside world. The receptionist handed me a note that read, "John C. Your parents are coming for Family Week."

I remember staring at the note for a long time. I sat down and cried. It was one of the most transformative moments in my whole process. *My parents are coming to see me? What?* Looking back on it now, it sounds ridiculous. I mean, *of course* my parents would have my back. They're good people. They're not monsters. But something deep inside me was constantly whispering, *If you don't perform, if you don't post funny videos, if you don't make people laugh, if you're a bad Christian, if you don't live up to the pearly image you portray, then you're worthless.* All that attention I'd been so desperate for was just a stand-in for the attention I really wanted, which was from my parents.

Look, I don't need my dad to throw a football with me in the yard now. I don't need my mom to look for my stolen bike. But the fact that they'd put their own lives on hold, that my dad, who was running for a Georgia State House seat, would pause his election campaign, that my mom would miss her school-board meetings, that they'd shelve everything and *show up* for me—that meant everything. It put the pin back in the grenade for me. I wasn't sure I'd ever have a career again, but at least I didn't feel as if the only way out of my circumstances was to jump off a cliff.

Shortly after all this, I made my first phone call from rehab, to my sister Emma. She, more than anyone, had a front-row seat to my fall from grace. She was one of my managers; she'd seen me on the road; she had the passwords to my social media accounts. I can't imagine how difficult it was for her to watch her big brother come apart at the seams. Not that I was thinking about any of that when we got on the phone. The very first thing I asked her was, "How many followers have I lost?" Even after all I'd been through, that was still the most important thing on my mind.

"None," she said.

Her answer floored me. I was shocked. Okay, maybe it was not exactly none, but for a guy with a million followers, it wasn't a noticeable amount. My fan base was largely intact. That confused me. I thought this was all conditional. I thought I had to maintain this facade for everyone to like me. Why were they still following me? I didn't get it.

Around this time, I started to receive mail. Not email but actual letters. Apparently, many years ago, people used to communicate this way. They'd write their thoughts on paper, put that paper in an envelope, affix a stamp, and then, magically, a few days later, their letter would arrive, often many miles away, at its chosen destination. It's an ingenious arrangement actually. Not sure what happened to it. I've heard the whole system is now devoted to making sure everyone in America has a never-ending supply of Bed Bath & Beyond coupons.

Anyway, at first the mail was a trickle. A letter from my brother, my mom, my aunt. It didn't matter what they said; just the idea that these people hadn't completely abandoned me was a revelation.

Mail became a lifeline. I developed a ritual around it to milk as much as I could from that lifeline. Every day around 2:00 P.M., if you had a letter, they'd write your name on a whiteboard. When there was a letter for me, I'd collect it, bring it to my room, and place it on my desk. At first, I wouldn't open it.

Merely knowing it existed made me feel better. Each letter represented some sort of faint possibility, the chance of a future different from the present I was enduring or the past I'd colossally screwed up. Once I'd read each letter, the magic started to wear off, so I'd usually put off reading it until the next morning, when that magic could be replaced by the hope of another letter coming that next day. After a while, there almost always was one.

In fact, I started getting stacks of letters. Mail is a real occasion in rehab, so this was a big deal. In these letters, people would unload their stories, and they were all the same. Friends, friends of friends, neighbors of friends of friends, anyone who'd ever been to the bottom seemed desperate to share their experience with me, to encourage me, to offer a ray of hope. People opened up about their worst failures—cheating on their spouses, losing their jobs, going to prison, becoming a drug addict—and reminded me of something I should've already known: We're all a mess; we all struggle; we all fall short, all the time. Every one of those letter writers emerged on the other side—maybe bruised and battered, but changed for the better.

I saved those letters because, at that moment, those letters saved me. It's like I was on a ventilator and each letter was a fresh whoosh of oxygen filling up my lungs. I was almost certainly being denounced in public, but privately, people understood. That meant something.

It began to dawn on me how wrong I'd been about so much and how good it felt to be wrong. I thought my family would abandon me. They didn't. I thought my friends would be ashamed of me. They weren't. I thought the rehab would tell me I was a lost cause. I wasn't. I figured every fan and follower would drop me. They didn't. I could see a light at the end of the tunnel, and I was pretty sure it wasn't an onrushing train.

During Family Week, one guy's wife approached me as we were walking out of a group-therapy session and pulled me aside.

"I've been a fan of yours for a long time," she said. "Your 'Millennial International' video is the funniest thing I've ever seen." Her talking to me about my life in the outside world was against the rules. I could immediately understand why. Just that one compliment gave me the kind of dopamine rush I'd been missing. I was high. Like *high* high. I could live without alcohol. I could live without the women. But I couldn't live without this. *This* was my addiction.

A NEW DEAL

The longer you're doing well in rehab, the more privileges you get. Again, the prison analogy rings true. The first night, they had two nurses on call and cameras that watched me sleep. After a couple of nights, they deemed I was at least reasonably stable, so they sent me to the dorm. Then I got my shoelaces and belt back. After about a month, I was allowed to leave campus to go to a local church.

The idea of going to church, the place at the center of my shame and downfall, made me feel *some* type of way. But people would know me at church. It was my drug. I could get a hit, and the rehab staff were oblivious to this. It'd feel great to soak up some recognition, but that would be significantly offset by the indignity of being seen disembarking from a van with "The Meadows Addiction Recovery Center" emblazoned on it. I re-member asking the driver where the van would pull up at the church. He assured me it was out of sight of the congregants, so I agreed to go. Clearly, I had some healing still to do.

At the beginning of the service, there was an opportunity to introduce yourself to the people around you. Typically, this is when everyone puts on their biggest, fakest smile, puffs out their chest, and tells everyone how amazing they're doing. "The job is going great!" you might crow, despite the fact that you're deathly afraid you're going to be laid off. "My son's basketball team just made the state finals!" someone will tell you, leaving out the fact that their son was suspended from the team because he was caught smoking weed after practice.

On that Sunday morning, I was fully prepared to honor this superficial tradition. A woman asked why I was in Wickenburg.

"Golfing trip with some buddies," I lied. "What about you?"

Apparently, she hadn't gotten the memo about the phony charade because she motioned to her friend sitting next to her and said, "We're at the Meadows' eating-disorder clinic."

I quickly came clean and explained that I was at the Meadows too. A guy sitting a row back then said, "I'm in the grief-and-loss center. My wife just died." An older man nearby was an alcoholic. For a moment, we unloaded a little of our struggles. We looked at one another as we were, flawed and hurting, and then, just like that, our loads seemed lighter. It felt better than church had felt in as long as I could remember.

Maybe *this* is what church was always supposed to be. It's not a gala reception for life's big winners. It's for the broken, the sick. I've been in a lot of megachurches with fog machines, flat-screen TVs, and light shows. But at many of these same places, if you go around back, next to the dumpster there's a door leading down a row of steps to a room with hard-backed folding chairs and lukewarm coffee. That's where the addiction-recovery groups meet. And if Jesus came back today, I bet he'd be more comfortable hanging out in the basement with the people in those folding chairs.

Without getting too pastory on you, I began to rethink my entire conception of God while I was in Wickenburg. I'd grown up imagining him as a disciplinarian enforcing a strict set of rules. In my mind, he was like a principal constantly calling me into his office, reviewing my behavior, and marking where I'd fallen short: *You stole a piece of candy; you looked at porn; you got drunk; you lied to that woman about your feelings.* But out there in the desert, my life in tatters, for the first time I started to think of God not as a distant, disappointed authority figure but as someone sitting right there beside me on a bench, looking out at the world.

"It's a real mess out there, huh?" I can almost hear him saying. "You're worried about your future. Maybe you'll never be able to work again. Maybe people will never forgive you. Maybe you'll never find someone to love you the way you need. All that would definitely suck. I get it. If you want to stay out here in Arizona, drink yourself to death, and fade away, that's fine. I still love you. But I'll tell you what: If you want to go back out and try to make it work, I'll go with you. It's going to be tough. You'll need to have a lot of uncomfortable conversations. You'll have to make a lot of amends. Some relationships may not be repairable. Some people won't want to hear from you. You're going to screw up again and again. And in the end, it may not work out the way you want. But if you want to try, I'll come with you."

It seemed a deal worth considering.

After a month at the Meadows, I could feel the life returning to my face. My family hadn't written me off. My career might even be recoverable. In the middle of this upturn, my room-mate found me walking down a trail toward dinner. I really liked this guy. He was in all sorts of pain, and we'd commiserate every night, alternately laughing and crying as we fell asleep. Anyway, he walked up, draped an arm around my shoulder, and looked at me with a solemn expression.

"I know you're doing great here," he said. "You've made so much progress. I've really seen the growth you've made as a person." He paused a second and looked deep into my eyes. "I want to say, from the bottom of my heart, don't take suicide off the table just yet."

That might have been the hardest I've laughed in my whole life.

THE FRIENDLY SKIES

People typically stay at the Meadows for forty-five days, and after I'd done my time, they decided I was free to go. When I was dropped off at the Phoenix airport, a monumental thing happened: They gave me my phone back. I'd already sat with a therapist and erased my internet history, any nude photos, and salacious text conversations. I even blocked and deleted phone numbers of people—mostly women and drinking buddies—who wouldn't be helpful to my recovery. Still, when I turned it on, it literally did not stop buzzing for an hour.

I found my gate and boarded my flight. As I walked on, one of the flight attendants recognized me and started crying. This was quite the reintroduction to the real world. Normally, if a flight attendant greets you like this, talk to her supervisor or maybe an air marshal about having her removed from the flight, but in this case, they were "good" tears. She reached out, hugged me, and said she'd been praying for me every day since she'd heard the news. I wasn't sure how the rest of the world would greet my reemergence, but at least one Southwest flight attendant was happy to see me.

A few weeks before I'd left the Meadows, the treatment team had recommended I go to what they called a step-down facility. Returning to the real world would be scary, so they wanted me to go someplace that could keep a close watch and make the transition easier. I followed their advice, flew back to Nashville, got in my car, and drove straight to a facility in Hattiesburg, Mississippi, called Pine Grove.

If the Meadows was like a prison, Pine Grove was like a half-way house. I had therapy and recovery programs from nine to five each day, but I had more freedom to do as I pleased in my off-hours. I could go out to dinner. I stayed in an off-campus apartment. I had my phone and my computer back, but we all agreed that it was best if I didn't get back on social media yet. I was ready to receive texts and calls from loved ones but not a barrage of anonymous strangers telling me I was the Antichrist or something like that.

I arrived there on Christmas Eve. Instead of gathering around a table with my family, eating my mom's cooking, while bright, cheery presents sat under a beautiful tree, I was in a metal fold-ing chair, eating cold cereal with a plastic spoon and playing Settlers of Catan with a bunch of addicts who'd burned their lives to the ground.

It was the best Christmas of my life.

I'm not kidding. Instead of doing what I normally do around

the holidays and put on some front for my family, telling them how great my life was going, how I'd just finished my biggest tour ever, how my video views were up, how many new followers I had on social media, and listening to my family members do something similar, I could just be the unholy mess that I really was. Everyone in there was so far past pretending they were something they weren't. It was as though the envy I'd had at that prison in Minnesota had finally been realized, and it was as good as I'd imagined. Also, I dominated Settlers of Catan! No lie.

THE FIRST RULE OF FIGHT CLUB

There's a big rehab community in Hattiesburg, and while I was there, we had to go to one public recovery meeting every day. I'd go to all types of meetings: Alcoholics Anonymous, Narcotics Anonymous, Depressed Anonymous, Sexaholics Anonymous. Whatever was available and fit into the schedule. I felt a bit like Ed Norton in *Fight Club,* although I wasn't getting a vicarious thrill through other people's pain in those meetings. I was just learning to be okay with being known for who I really was by being around people who already were.

It was like the opposite of my old life. Before, I wanted to present the best side of myself. To make sure everyone on the internet knew I was perfect. Now I was in rehab, going to meetings, hanging out with a bunch of addicts. But I didn't care. I didn't care if people saw me or took photos of me. I had nothing to hide anymore, no facade to defend.

I was also allowed to go to church while I was at Pine Grove. I'd spotted a big megachurch when I first drove into town, the kind of place where people would definitely know me. I wish I could say I wanted to go there because I was eager to worship among fellow believers, but to be honest, I wanted the ego boost. So one Sunday, a few of us from Pine Grove made plans to attend. One was a guy I'd met who was constantly making comments about which women at the facility he wanted to sleep with and telling me stories about partying. He wasn't religious at all, so I was surprised he wanted to go. But he got all dressed up and even brought a big Bible with him.

Right after the service, the two women sitting in front of us turned around and asked if I was John Crist. *Ah, yes, just what I came for: the old familiar drug.* I flirted a little, took a photo with them, and introduced them to this guy I'd come with, then walked toward the parking lot. I glanced back to see that my friend was still talking with these women. Eventually, one gave him her phone number. When he caught up with me, he immediately started talking about how he was going to hook up with this hot chick who'd given him her number. I was furious. Here he was, walking into church, carrying his Bible, pretending he was a good Christian, when all he wanted was to get with this girl. He completely misled her about who he really was. It all made me furious. I was literally ready to fight this guy in the parking lot.

When I calmed down and talked with my therapist the next day, it occurred to me why I was so pissed: There before the grace of God go I. He was me—pretending I was someone I was not, pretending I was a good Christian, to convince women to be with me. I'd just never seen what it looked like from the outside. It wasn't pretty.

After I talked through that whole church visit with my therapist and how it fed my addiction to be known and loved, she banned me from church. That's right. I'm probably the only person in the history of rehab that was banned from church.

If I couldn't get my fix in church, I quickly identified the next best place: Chick-fil-A. The first time I went into a Chick-fil-A in Hattiesburg, people were taking photos and telling me how much they loved my work. It was amazing! Maybe you can guess what happened next. Yup, my therapist banned me from Chick-fil-A too. So, if you're keeping track at home, there I am in rehab, and the two places that I'm banned from in Hattiesburg aren't the liquor store and the strip club; they're church and Chick-fil-A.

That's the kind of treatment center it was: very honest, no punches pulled. There was one guy in there who kind of became famous for his cooking. Every weekend, we'd go over to his place and he'd cook these huge spreads. We looked forward to it the entire week. All we talked about was how good his cooking was.

They banned him from cooking.

This other guy was really rich. Every Saturday, he'd go to the local car dealership, test-drive cars, and get fawned over.

They banned him from going to the car dealership.

Look, eating at Chick-fil-A isn't a problem. Cooking for your friends isn't a problem. Test-driving a car isn't a problem. But for each of us, *the way* we did these things were definite problems.

We were all looking to conjure up some new source of worth, of affirmation, a way to receive love. You don't need to be an addict to get that. Everyone has something they do to make them feel valued and loved. If you're lucky, your attachment to it is healthier than mine. Look at what I do for a living: I literally *have* to perform to get validation in return. That seems like an unhealthy transaction, especially if it is a deal I'm going to make over and over for the rest of my life. Surely, there's a better way.

20

RETURN OF THE LIVING DEAD

I'd planned to stay at Pine Grove for six weeks, but in the end, I stayed for twelve. I felt comfortable there, but eventually the staff began nudging me toward the exit, the way parents might encourage a recent college grad still sleeping in his childhood bedroom and eating his mom's cooking that maybe it's time to move out. The whole world was still out there, and I needed to face it sooner or later.

I left Hattiesburg in early March 2020 and returned to Nashville. I didn't have plans to do much, which worked out well because a few weeks later, Covid-19 shut the whole world down. I don't mean to make light of a once-in-a-century public health tragedy, but I will say that while everyone else was struggling to adapt to new restrictions on their lives, I was pretty much fine. In fact, this was more freedom than I'd had in months! Sure, I couldn't go to the comedy club for a while, but I could eat all the Chick-fil-A and play all the golf I wanted. I was living the dream. I felt like Andy Dufresne at the end of *Shawshank Redemption,* except instead of crawling through a sewer to escape a prison in Maine, I drove my Honda out of an apartment complex in Hattiesburg. So, yeah, totally the same.

Back in Nashville, I was very deliberate about putting my life back together piece by piece. I reconnected with friends and family. I quit drinking. Booze was a way for me to lower my inhibitions and impair my judgment—I mean, those are pretty much alcohol's biggest selling points—so at least for now, I feel like I need to avoid it.

After a while, I started to consider posting again on social media. That would be a big step forward, but I knew I couldn't just show back up after months of silence and be like, "So, what's the deal with quarantine, huh?" So many people had been asking, "Where's John?" "What's been going on with John?"

After about four months of being home, I posted a video explaining it all and thanking the people whose support helped keep me alive. I knew that video was going to be the place where people would be able to get off their chests whatever they wanted to say about me. If they were mad, if they felt betrayed or hurt, if they wanted to tell a story about me, or if they wanted to show their support, they could do so in the comments section. And it was important to me that no matter what people said, I wasn't going to delete those comments. I wasn't going to block anyone. Instead of trying to hide things or manipulate a narrative about who I was, it was all going to be out there for everyone to see.

When the video posted, the comments were overwhelmingly positive, but there were certainly people who unloaded on me. That stuff is still up. Nothing is hidden. It's genuinely liberating to know that everything is out in the open. There's nothing I'm afraid of people finding out about me. The darkness had come into the light, and it held no more power. If that's not a Bible verse, it sure sounds like one.

The very next video I posted was maybe the riskiest thing I've ever posted. It was me walking through the supermarket, clowning on all the products that needed to be "canceled." ("PAW Patrol Mac & Cheese? Defund the police. Defund PAW Patrol!") Of course, I had basically just been canceled myself, so by posting that video, I was pretty much asking for people to lay into me. But if I wasn't going to say the unsayable, what's the point? It turned out to be the biggest video of my entire career.

There's no way I would've posted something like that prior to being in rehab. It would've been "off brand." Not Christian. Not unchristian, but certainly not overtly Christian. But the video is definitely the way that I think. And if, as a comedian, I'm not going to share the way I actually think, then what am I doing this for? I finally felt free to joke about whatever I wanted.

To be clear, there were plenty of people who crushed me for that video. I wouldn't go as far as to say that reading that stuff doesn't bother me at all—of course it does—but it doesn't paralyze me anymore. It doesn't send me spiraling in shame. It doesn't make me start thinking about hurling myself off a nearby bridge. My self-worth is no longer wrapped up in what the internet thinks about me. I'm not living in fear that once my fans find out who I *really* am, they're going to hate me. It's all out there, and whatever happens is not going to change what *I* think about me.

Listen, I know that to this day there are a bunch of people with a bunch of different opinions of me—all of which, I totally understand. "You should go away and never come back." "Your apology wasn't good enough." "Ye without sin cast the first stone." "Ignore the haters and just keep going." "You don't need to apologize to anyone." I've heard them all. A lot of what is written or said about me is true. A lot is untrue. Agree or disagree with my actions or words, no doubt women were hurt by the way I acted. And that makes me sad. As an influential person, a Christian, a man, and a human being, I wish I would have behaved differently, communicated more clearly. But I didn't. Do I regret that? Yes. Am I sorry for that? Absolutely. Am I trying to do better now? Without a doubt.

GOOGLE ME

Once I was back out in the world again, I met someone I was interested in. She wasn't a fan, and I hadn't met her at a show or in my DMs; she was a friend of a friend. I was attracted to her and thought we'd have fun together, but I also felt like she was out of my league. There was a time when I wouldn't have had the confidence to put myself out there to possibly be rejected by her. I used to lean hard on my comedy and ask out only women who knew who I was and who likely wouldn't turn me down. This woman was none of those things, but I asked her to dinner, and just the asking itself felt really good. It felt even better when she said yes. I felt inspired; I felt confident; I had this surge of positive and, frankly, unfamiliar emotions.

We went out together and had fun. In fact, we had such a great time that we went to lunch together the very next day, and it was even better. We talked about all sorts of things, but my personal life, the things I'd been through during the previous year or so—none of that came up. A few days later, she was with her family and texted me to say that they were sitting around watching my videos. At that moment, I felt an instant, familiar rush of shame. When we were just getting to know each other on first dates, it didn't seem like the time to bring up the darkest moments in my personal life. (Watch one episode of *The Bachelor,* and you'll see that's not a good idea.) But now that this woman was essentially introducing me to her family as this guy she's dating, she needs to know. Because if she googles me, she's going to find out anyway.

I texted her and told her that I'd had a great time with her but wanted her to know that I'd been through a lot in my personal life, much of which had been made public. If we were going to continue dating and she was going to introduce me to her family and such, she should know all those things about me. If my past was too much or made her uncomfortable and she felt that we shouldn't date anymore, I'd understand. She texted me back to say that she already knew about all that stuff but she believed in second chances and forgiveness.

I started crying when I got that text message back from her. (Okay, I was crying pretty easily in the months after rehab!) I thought, *This is what it feels like to be open and honest with people, to be the real you in public and private.* It reminded me of meeting those people at church when I was at the Meadows.

The relationship with that woman didn't end up going anywhere, but that interaction was still meaningful. Carrying secrets is tough, man. Rehab was filled with people who'd hidden the messier parts of their lives—addictions, infidelities, mistakes, crimes—for so long. Those secrets bred shame. That hiding is a burden no human is equipped to carry. But being in rehab, around people who knew all my secrets but still loved me, helped me shed that load, brick by brick. Do I still make bad choices? Absolutely! But it doesn't grip me anymore. A bad choice doesn't make me a bad person. That shame used to absolutely consume me. It doesn't anymore.

One day in rehab, a guy broke down and told us that he paid for his girlfriend to get an abortion in high school. More than *twenty* years earlier. He'd been holding that secret for more than twenty years, thinking if he ever told anyone, they'd shame him. That's a long time to live in a mental prison. This man cried and cried that day, and you could just about see the twenty years of shame slowly lifting off his shoulders. The irony is, when he finally unburdened himself, the reaction was the opposite of what he'd always feared: We felt *closer* to him, more deeply connected to him. I experienced situations like that over and over in rehab.

I *want* people to know the real me. If that means someone isn't going to be my fan anymore, that's okay. Sometimes I feel like Eminem in that final rap-battle scene in *8 Mile*. He says every bad thing about himself, and then the other rapper has no ammunition to use against him. It's powerful. A company recently wanted me to do a sponsored video for their brand. I told my manager to make sure they knew *everything* I'd been through over the past year. If they still wanted to work with me, great. If not, fine. They emailed back the next day, thanked us for telling them, and still wanted to proceed. Wait, WHAT? It was the same feeling as when my parents visited me at rehab or that Southwest flight attendant hugged me. Since rehab, my life has been a steady procession of these "Wait, WHAT?" experiences—at restaurants, at church, at shows. Everything I thought I knew about humanity turns out not to be true. I've never been so happy to be wrong.

MEASURING SUCCESS

I'm healthier now, but let's be clear: I'm not healthy. I don't imagine there's a finish line I'll one day cross in the race toward emotional well-being. It's the work itself that is the best sign that you're moving in the right direction.

This need for public affirmation, this trouble I have in constantly seeking it out, can be a tough thing to keep track of. Unlike with alcoholism or drug addiction, there's no simple daily baseline metric for how I'm doing. At Alcoholics Anonymous, they give out tokens to mark however many days it's been since your last drink. Nobody's giving out tokens for using the Chick-fil-A drive-through instead of going inside for an ego boost. There's no congratulatory chip ceremony for not checking how many views my last video got. No one bakes me a cake to celebrate when I refrain from responding to some woman who DMs me a nude photo. (That would be a weird call to the Kroger cake department. "Okay, you want your cake to say *what*?") There's no triumphant postgame press conference for not liking a thirst-trap video at 1:00 A.M. Maybe there should be: "You know what, it was tough. I was having a rough night, feeling insecure. The girl I was supposed to go out with tonight backed out, so I wasn't feeling great about myself. I was scrolling TikTok because I couldn't sleep. That wasn't in the game plan today, but you know, it was a game-time decision. I mean, sure, I watched the video of the woman dancing in a bikini for longer than I probably should've, but at the end of the day, I refrained from DMing her and got out of there with a big win."

I'm still in an industry that equates success with fame, and fame with self-worth, so trying to uncouple those two things in my psyche may not be entirely possible. I still love making videos and telling jokes. But something important has shifted. I love that people like my videos and share them, but I don't neeeeeed it like I used to. I don't put my self-worth in the hands of some strangers behind a screen or in an audience.

To get to here, I had to lose everything, at least in *my* mind. I had to be at peace with never being able to do comedy again, never standing on a stage, never having another video go viral. I had to learn to be okay with the "John C" who was just a guy, a son, a brother, a friend, an uncle, a future husband. Because if I'm looking to extract all my validation as a human being from career success, from social media followers, from standing ovations, man, I'm going to wind up right back on a metal folding chair in Wickenburg playing Settlers of Catan. Or someplace worse.

21

TAG ME

I was chatting with a woman recently who I'd met at a show. I started following her on Instagram and then, of course, scrolled back through her posts to get a sense of who she was—or, at least, who she was trying to be. There was nothing too scandalous in the photos, but I did start noticing the same guy, over and over. The two of them at dinner. The two of them, cheeks pressed together, mugging for a selfie. The two of them arm in arm at a party. So I asked her straight up, "Are you dating this guy?"

She hemmed and hawed a little bit. "Well, yeah, it's kind of an off-and-on thing. It's complicated. But can we just keep any mention of you and me kind of quiet for the moment?"

When she told me that, I could feel my neck stiffen and my gut clench. She and I hadn't done anything wrong, there was nothing to be ashamed of, but in that moment, that simple request for discretion, I could feel the dread of living a life of secrets come roaring back. I remember that old life, and it ain't fun.

As a homeschooled Southern Christian, I'd grown up trying

to keep so many secrets, about things big and small. Make sure your grandma doesn't find out you got detention. Make sure your youth pastor doesn't find out you looked at porn. Make sure the church doesn't find out you drink. Make sure your girlfriend doesn't find out you're texting someone else. It never ends. I'm not saying I've got to share every inch of my life with the world—because, for sure, the world is not interested in every inch of my life—but these days, I'm at least trying to err on the side of openness. Which can occasionally make for some interesting scenes:

I went to Walgreens a while back to fill a prescription, and the pharmacy tech recognized me when I got to the front of the line.

"Hey, you're John Crist," he said. "Bro, I love you. You're so funny. I love the lightness that you bring to all your videos. It really brightens my days."

"Thanks, man."

"So, how can I help you?"

I paused for a second and shrugged. "I'm here to pick up my antidepressants."

For most of my life, I never could've imagined uttering that sentence in public. When I was in rehab, I resisted getting on antidepressants. On one level, I was afraid the medication would numb me out and mess with my ability to be funny or creative. But it was more than that. My whole life I'd been taught that if I wasn't acting right, if I was feeling sad, I just needed to pray harder and read the Bible more. Antidepressants felt like an unchristian admission of failure, of imperfection. I mean, there was a time when I untagged myself from a photo in that exact same Walgreens because I was buying anti-itch cream. Antidepressants seemed a lot more serious than that. But I didn't really care anymore. If people didn't want to accept me or like me anymore because I was on antidepressants, that was fine with me.

So dropping the pretenses and just owning up to who I really was felt good. After all I'd been through, after all I'd put other people through, here I was, smiling and declaring to this guy working the register and to everyone in line at the pharmacy that day, "Hey, I'm broken. I'm not okay all the time." And nearly every time I've admitted my many imperfections to anyone, they typically respond, "Saaaaaaame."

BETTER BUT NOT "GOOD"

I was driving through downtown Nashville recently on my way to a meeting when suddenly, in the middle of the day, traffic ground to a halt. I craned my neck out the window of my car, and I could see at the intersection up ahead what looked like a mass of people marching down the street in some sort of protest. I had no idea what they were protesting, but as I sat there, I was feeling good and thinking, *Man, what a great country we live in, where you have the freedom to gather with like-minded people in the street and stand up for whatever cause you believe in.* A patriotic glow washed over me, even as I sat there in traffic, my car not moving an inch.

That glow lasted about ten minutes. That was the point when I realized these protesters, or whatever they were, were going to make me late for my meeting. After twenty minutes, new thoughts started creeping into my head: *How many people do they really need in this march to make their point? Wouldn't their protest be just as effective in an open field, somewhere where they wouldn't be inconveniencing random strangers?* Once thirty minutes had passed, my entire attitude had changed. I didn't know what this demonstration was all about, but whatever they were for, I was hard-core against. I was sitting there in the driver's seat, stewing and plotting a long-term campaign to undermine whatever their cause was. Screw these people and their rights! I've got places to be!

After nearly forty-five minutes, traffic started to move. I was steamed. As I crossed the intersection where the traffic was blocked, I looked around to try to figure out what they'd been marching for, what important principle had been worth making me miss my meeting. It turned out that it wasn't a protest march at all. It was a half marathon. Go figure.

I guess what I'm saying is that even after all the work I've done on myself, the line for me between being a high-minded, noble soul and an angry, vindictive narcissist is a lot thinner than I sometimes would like to admit. I think that's the same for many of us.

Not too long ago, I got on a flight from the West Coast back to Nashville. This flight had been delayed twice, so it was nearly 1:00 A.M. by the time we all settled into our seats. Everyone was bleary eyed, exhausted, and ready to pass out for the duration of the trip. Just after they'd closed the boarding doors, I heard someone's emotional-support dog bark a few rows away from me. It wasn't that loud, but everyone around me on the plane heard it too, and there was an outpouring of warm comments. "Oh, he's so cute!" "What's his name?" "Can I pet him?"

Then as the flight was taxiing out to the runway, he barked again, this time a little louder. A few people nodded and smiled at the dog's owner, but the mushy feelings toward this animal were definitely waning. By the time the plane was in the air and the dog was barking and growling up a storm, most of the exhausted passengers were shooting angry looks at the dog's owner and muttering to their travel companions about how she'd probably gotten a fake doctor's note in order to get the "emotional support" collar. (By the way, if you suffer from anxiety, how does bringing a barking dog onto a plane filled with three hundred passengers who want to sleep help to *alleviate* that anxiety?) By mid-flight, I think most of us were plotting that dog's quick demise. I know I was. Look, I want to be a kind, sympathetic human, and I certainly want the world to believe I'm one, but just beneath the surface lurks a monster who has Animal Control on speed dial.

Because I grew up outside Atlanta, when the Braves made it to the World Series in 2021, I went. No question. I went and paid to sit in the front, near the dugout. #canthidemoney. Between innings, one of the ball boys came over and tossed a ball to a little boy sitting a few rows in front of me. It was a sweet gesture to give this boy, who was probably about six, a souvenir to remember the game by forever. Except that this six-year-old did what six-year-olds often do when you throw a ball at them: He dropped it. And when he did, a middle-aged guy a few seats away opportunistically grabbed the ball and pocketed it. I get it: This is the *World Series*! Everyone in the section quickly began booing and yelling at the older dude to give the kid the ball. And I get that impulse. But you know what a part of me was thinking? *Kid should've caught that ball. Honestly, kid, be better.* His dad could use this as a teaching moment. Do these types of thoughts make me a bad person, or just an honest one?

Those aren't warm-fuzzy thoughts, but they're real. They are still part of me. Remember when I was telling you about Ray Rice, the former Baltimore Ravens' star running back who was seen on video punching his fiancée in an elevator and knocking her out cold? When it happened, I was absolutely disgusted and probably voiced that disgust to plenty of people. But I'm ashamed to admit that right after he was cut by the Ravens, my next thought was a little less generous: *Yeah, I know he's a problematic dude, but man, the Falcons sure could use a good running back.*

This is all part of the distance between who we are, who we claim to be, and who we aim to be. In a perfect world, all three of those would be the same. But this is not a perfect world, and none of us are perfect people. We all love the WNBA *in theory,* but how many of us really sit and watch WNBA games? It takes a lot of work, a lot of patience, a lot of selflessness, to try to be your "best self." Accepting that I'm not always going to live up to that mark, that I'm hopelessly flawed, has been a huge relief for me.

Have you seen all the memes of LeBron James reading books? It seems wherever he is—in the locker room, at a press conference, courtside during practice—he's always toting some impressive-looking book with him: *The Autobiography of Malcolm X, The Alchemist,* or *The Tipping Point.* He always seems to be on the first chapter of that book too. On one level, it's nice that LeBron wants to show the world he's well-read. It's nice that books have become a peculiar sort of status symbol. I certainly won't complain if I see footage of him leaving the Staples Center holding this book. But on another level, I want to yell to LeBron and say, "Dude, you don't have to try so hard to impress us. You're the greatest player of your generation. You're an entrepreneur. You're a philanthropist. We love you already." Trying to keep up appearances is exhausting. I know.

FIRST CHURCH OF BABY-BACK RIBS

Speaking of basketball, when my beloved Atlanta Hawks played the Philadelphia 76ers in the playoffs in 2021, I went to the game with some buddies. One of the Sixers' best players, Ben Simmons, was having a tough game—a tough playoffs, honestly. He was passing up open shots. He was turning the ball over uncharacteristically. A real case of the yips. The fans quickly picked up on this and really let him have it. The whole crowd was chanting, "Ben Simmons sucks! Ben Simmons sucks!" I was yelling it too. On the court, Simmons looked crestfallen. I could see it. I witnessed it with my own eyes.

About an hour and a half after the game ended, I was walking back to my car alone through downtown Atlanta and I started to think about that chant again. At the time, Simmons was a twenty-four-year-old guy who was good at basketball but having a really bad day. Sixteen thousand people were not only enjoying that bad day but also reveling in making it worse for him. I know that people will say, "Hey, he's an NBA player; he's making millions; this is part of the deal," and sure it is. But I still couldn't help thinking that as I walked back toward my car, within a mile or so of where I stood, Simmons was probably alone, in his hotel room, laying his head on his pillow and scrolling through Twitter on his phone, seeing fans pile on and compound his misery. I felt bad for my part in it.

The fact that Simmons ended up sitting out the following season as he dealt with mental-health issues certainly drove all this home later, but I had no idea about any of that on the night of the game. Something about going through what I went through and being in rehab, though, changed my perspective on this stuff. It's made it hard not to put myself in other people's shoes. It's made it hard for me to pass judgment on people from afar. I am moved to empathy much quicker than ever before. And I think that's a good thing.

Empathy is easy in the abstract but less so in the real world. We're pretty much conditioned as humans to put our own selfish needs first, whether those needs are to get to a meeting on time, get some sleep on a late-night flight, enjoy the thrill and power of being part of a crowd, or anything else. I think, as humans, that's our default setting: selfish.

Empathy, on the other hand, takes work. It takes experience. It takes knowing what it feels like to be the victim of someone else's quest for self-gratification, understanding what it is to be the person who messed up, and being able to access all that in a moment when your own selfish instincts are pushing you in the opposite direction. In this way, I think empathy is something we work toward, not something we ever fully achieve. If my experiences over the past few years have taught me anything, it's that although we're all pretty different on the surface—although we might belong to different political parties, believe in different religions, support different sports teams, or wear different clothes—deep down we're more similar than we think.

I grew up going to my church (my dad's church, really) and believing *that* church was the one with all the right answers. Of course, in order to get to that church, I had to drive past thirty churches whose congregants thought they were the ones with all the right answers. But I was always taught that those other churches were wrong or misguided, that the people who attended them were weird or uneducated, that they were too liberal or too conservative or too *something*. I figured the people at those churches weren't like me; they were *other*. That's just how I was raised.

The spiritual journey I've been on has opened me up to the idea that maybe I don't know what I thought I knew. I found it easier to see things from other people's point of view. And in doing so, I got curious about other churches, so I started checking them out. And there were definitely things that were different from what I was used to.

I went to an Anglican church, and for communion everyone kneeled at the front and the priest put communion bread into their mouths. That wasn't how it was done at my church. I visited an Eastern Orthodox church, and that was a trip. When I walked in, they gave me a candle that I was supposed to light and put in this sandbox-looking thing. The clergyman who led the service was wearing a long frock, and some kids carried these little contraptions that spewed smoke. I went to an Amish church, and it was very austere. All the women wore head coverings and dresses. No musical instruments were allowed. The parking lot was filled with carriages and bicycles. At a cowboy church a couple of hours south of Nashville, there was a hitching post outside the front door and they did baptisms in a horse trough, took the offering in a cowboy hat, and had a guy playing the steel guitar.

All that stuff was very different from what I grew up with, and at times I was uncomfortable. I remember trying to follow along with the service at the Eastern Orthodox church and just being utterly lost. Then some guy in khakis and a button-down shirt who looked just like someone I might be friends with saw that I looked confused and offered some help. "Hey, man, my name is Brad. We're on page thirty-seven. We're going to read here, then we'll all recite this verse, then we're going to do two songs, and then the priest is going to do this. Let me know if you need anything." After the service, he asked me if I wanted to go to Chili's with him and a few other guys to watch the Titans game. The religious tradition may have been nothing I was used to, but the after-church tradition was right in my wheelhouse.

It was the same at the other places too. Wherever I went, people were welcoming, and most seemed to know who I was. Even at the Amish church, people came up to me afterward and said, "Hey, we really love your videos!" which was a bit confusing since I thought the Amish didn't have cellphones or computers, but apparently some of them do. Who am I to judge? Was it weird that every dude at cowboy church had a gun on his hip? I mean, yeah, that's different than the church I grew up in, but after the service, I was quickly invited to a potluck dinner and encouraged to try Aunt Evelyn's fried chicken, which I'm happy to report was unbelievable. So, again, yes, it was different, but when you dig a little deeper, not really. Some people kneel to pray, some people stand up, sometimes there's a pastor, sometimes there's a priest, sometimes there's an offering plate, sometimes there's a cowboy hat, but at the end of the day, everyone is just yearning for a community and a place to belong. Aside from Chili's, of course.

TRIP TO THE STORE

Back in 2014, I moved to Los Angeles. I thought of it back then as a savvy career move, and on the surface, it made some sense.

I'd already climbed the comedy-club ladder in Denver and had established myself as a pretty decent draw across Middle America. The next step was to go to Hollywood and become a big star, right? Except that around L.A., I was a nobody. My fans weren't there, and the entertainment industry didn't know who I was. That wasn't something I discovered when I got there. I knew it before I went. So why go? Why essentially start over on a career that seemed to be going just fine? What was I looking for in L.A.?

I started hanging around the Comedy Store in West Hollywood. For those of you who aren't familiar with it, for a stand-up comic, the Comedy Store is holy ground. The club, which got its start in the early seventies, helped launch or mold the careers of Richard Pryor, Robin Williams, Sam Kinison, Jay Leno, David Letterman, and Jim Carrey, among others. It's not uncommon for superstars like Dave Chappelle or Chris Rock to just drop in to work on new material. To have your name painted on the wall of the Comedy Store is like being knighted. It's an acknowledgment from the comedy gods that you have made it.

So, what did I want in L.A.? For starters, my name on that wall. When I walked in there, though, I had to get in line with all the other open mic-ers. No one cared that I was packing theaters in Texas. No one cared that my videos were getting millions of views. This led to a pretty schizophrenic existence. On weekends, I'd leave town to perform in front of rabid sold-out crowds across Middle America, and then I'd return to L.A., where I'd spend Monday, Tuesday, and Wednesday at the Store trying to get onstage to do two minutes for free in front of whoever was there at two in the morning. There I was just another new guy hanging around, hoping to get my chance. The whole situation felt bizarre, but I was desperate for the validation of the comedy elite. The attention and affection of the people who I knew liked me just weren't enough. It went on like that for a few years. Finally, around 2017, one of the Store regulars, a comic named Andrew Santino, pulled me aside and posed a very good question.

"Hey, dude, what are you doing here?" I'd become friendly with Andrew, and he knew about my fan base and my videos. "You pack out theaters. People love you. Any one of these comics around here would kill to have what you have. Why are you here? You're going to hang around the Store for six or seven years, you'll finally become a regular, you'll get your name on the wall, and then you'll walk into the greenroom and realize that there's nothing here for you." In essence, he was saying, *Trust me, man. This place cannot give you what you're ultimately striving for.* He was like some kind of stand-up-comedy prophet to me at that moment.

He didn't mean any of that as an insult, to me or the Store, and I didn't take it as one. In fact, it was a great piece of advice. But when I think back on it now and try to understand why I was out in L.A., trying to impress people who didn't care about me, I realize it's because that's what I've been doing for my whole adult life. That's why I became a comedian in the first place. I keep chasing after validation, thinking that it will fill up the emptiness inside me, and when it doesn't, I start looking for it someplace else. My therapist in Hattiesburg said it was like I was walking around desperately trying to fill a cup that had a huge hole in the bottom. I could really relate to that.

I feel the same way about the Comedy Store that I do about

The Tonight Show. Culturally, *The Tonight Show* may not have the importance that it once did, but I grew up watching my favorite stand-ups on that show. For a comic like me, performing on *The Tonight Show* is the ultimate in career success. Everyone who thought I'd never make it, every girl who ever turned me down, everyone who overlooked or ignored me—I'd always thought that if I walked out onstage to perform on *The Tonight Show,* all those wrongs would be righted. But would they?

Imagine there was a comic and all he ever wanted was to be on *The Tonight Show.* He worked hard in his twenties and got really good. Auditioned in his thirties but didn't get the show. Worked harder, toured more, came back, and auditioned in his forties. Didn't get it. Tried again in his fifties. No luck. Finally, after all these years, he gets his shot to be on *The Tonight Show* at age sixty-five. He rehearses his lines, prepares the best he knows how to, and strides out onto that stage. He does his four and a half minutes of comedy and walks off. It goes great. He kills. There is that rush that he always imagined, and it's sweet. And then it's over. He walks outside, it's three-thirty in the afternoon—that's when those late shows tape—and he's on the curb of a studio in Burbank, waiting on his Uber. His life is the same. Maybe the rush lasts a little longer, but it wears off. And that bottomless pit inside him is still not full. That wasn't the magic elixir he thought it was going to be. So now what?

Success in anything is often compared to a mountain that you climb, but what they don't tell you is that the mountain does not have a summit. Just as you reach what you thought would be the top, a cloud clears and you see that you still have so much more to climb. (Shout-out to Miley Cyrus.) I remember when I first started doing comedy, people would ask me, "Do you get paid?" *Well, not yet.* Then when I got paid a little, the question was, "Do you do it full time?" *Not yet.* Then I quit my day job. "Do you ever tour?" *Not yet.* Then I started to tour. "Are you ever on TV?" *Not yet.* Then I was on TV. You see where this is going. *It never ends.*

If the past few years and the process of writing this book have taught me anything, it's that I can't keep looking outside myself to find the thing that's going to fix what's inside myself. What happened to me, having my life turned upside down in public, was horrible, excruciating, and embarrassing. I wouldn't wish it on my worst enemy, really and truly. But the only thing I can imagine being worse is if it had never happened. I'd have just kept on aimlessly spinning the hamster wheel (no offense to hamsters and the entire rodent community): I give you videos; you give me likes. I make you laugh; you mask my insecurities. In rehab, there's a term for this: It's called codependence.

THE BIG TRADE

I quit drinking after I went to rehab. (I mean, that's kind of what rehab is for, right?) I don't know if I'm an alcoholic, but I do know that drinking had contributed to some bad choices in my life, and it was easier to avoid making those same choices again if I was sober. It's possible I might get to a point in my life when it feels okay to have a glass of wine or a beer with dinner, but who knows? For now, I'm better off without the booze.

I'm really careful about how I talk about drinking, though, because the last thing I want is to become someone who is loudly and proudly declaring my sobriety to the world. The issue for me is not the sobriety so much as it is creating a public image that I then need to live up to.

I still go out to bars, clubs, and shows all the time. When I'm out, I almost always order a sugar-free Red Bull on ice. That's my favorite thing to drink (and it has been for a long time), which, health-wise, is probably way worse for you than a beer, but that's not the point of this story. It normally comes in a clear cup or a glass with a cocktail straw. To anyone who doesn't know, it could easily look like a vodka Red Bull—same color. For years, back when I was trying to live up to my reputation as every evangelical's favorite Christian, I got really good at hiding my drink in photos. Just before someone would snap a picture, I'd carefully slide it behind a friend's back or nudge it out of the frame. Sometimes those drinks didn't even have alcohol in them, but I was forever in fear of being tagged in some photo even appearing to be drinking alcohol.

But now, I guess, I'm free. Or at least I feel free. When someone pulls out their phone to take a photo, my gut doesn't clench up. I don't make a mental note to check social media later on so I can untag myself from the photo. I don't fear anyone calling me out anymore, because I'm no longer pretending to be something I'm not. And if you do see a picture of me holding a Red Bull or anything else, and your moral code doesn't allow you to support someone who appears to consume alcohol, then that's fine too. You can unfollow me, and we can part ways amicably. No harm done.

In 2021, I got my chip for being two years sober. If you're in recovery, these chips are a big deal, kind of a physical embodiment of the progress you've made and the commitment you've kept. I felt great about it, and when I got home, I took a photo of the chip and sent it to some of the people closest to me.

Then I thought about posting that photo on social media.

With what I'd been through, I knew that post of the two-year chip would be huge. It would be the biggest hitter on my page. People would invite me on their podcasts to talk about it. Churches would ask me to come speak to their youth groups. All the publications that wrote about my cancellation in 2019 would likely write about my redemption. The affirmation would feel amazing. And all for doing something good.

But nothing in this world comes without a price. And the price of posting a photo of that chip is that I would become John Crist, Professional Sober Person. I'd have to start thinking harder about those photos of me with the Red Bull. If in a moment of weakness I had a vodka and Sprite or if I just decided one day that I was okay with having a beer, I'd immediately have to start untagging myself from photos again. I'd have to go back into the darkness, into the secret life, because I'd told everyone that I was sober. I'd have to work to keep certain people in the dark about my drinking, shots in the bathroom and such. Doing that, you start constructing this architecture of shame. I read a quote recently that really hit home: "The greater the facade, the greater the shadow." I don't want to live in the shadows anymore.

In the end, not posting that chip photo was important for me. I had to trade the hit, trade the endorphin rush, for a shot at long-term mental health. I don't think that's a trade I would've been able to make just a few years ago.

Remember way back near the beginning of this book when I was talking about those email notifications that Facebook sends when you've been tagged in a photo, and the way we all immediately log on to check them out? I was worse about that than anyone. When I'd get one of those notifications, it didn't matter what I was doing, didn't matter where I was—I could be driving, I could be in a deep emotional conversation with a friend, I could be at a fancy dinner with my parents, I could literally be *at* the movie theater—I was going to drop everything and immediately go see that photo I was tagged in.

Well, going to rehab and working on myself doesn't mean I'm suddenly immune to those impulses. It doesn't mean that I don't care at all about what people think of me. We're all human, and we all care. But I don't care nearly as much as I once did. I don't have anything to hide anymore, so it no longer matters that much what people find out about me. Now when one of those notifications comes in while I'm driving, it can wait until I get home. If I get one while I'm in a movie theater, it can wait until after the credits roll. If my phone pings just as I'm drifting off to bed, I can sleep soundly knowing that my Facebook notifications will be there waiting for me in the morning.

That feels like progress.

STAND AND SALUTE

Around 2012, I did a comedy tour for the troops in Kuwait. It was a great opportunity for me. Granted, they were *our* troops, which made it a little friendlier of an audience. A guy had seen me perform at a club, thought I was funny, and asked me if I wanted to go on the tour, along with two other comics. At the time, I wasn't totally deserving of the opportunity, but I guess I ticked some boxes for them: My material was clean, it was largely apolitical, and I didn't talk too much about relationships, which not surprisingly can be a trigger for soldiers stuck in the desert away from their loved ones for sixteen months at a time.

The tour was life changing for me. We were based at Camp Arifjan, a giant military complex near Kuwait, and each day we'd drive a few hours into the desert to other bases, where we'd put on shows. We'd ride in armored vehicles, and when we'd roll through a town or village, they'd often block off an intersection, presumably to guard against an ambush, though truth be told, this was Kuwait, not Iraq, so the chance of any actual violence was basically nil. I also can't imagine that as a comedian hardly anyone had ever heard of, I would be a particularly high-value target: "Did you see his YouTube video about texting and driving? We've gotta take this man down!" Nonetheless, I was treated like visiting royalty there, and it quickly occurred to me that it must have cost a fortune to bring us across the globe to tell jokes. I asked one of the commanding officers how they justified the expense. He looked at me and said something that I will never ever *ever* forget. He said, "When the comedians come over, the suicide rate goes down." *When the comedians come over, the suicide rate goes down. When the comedians come over, the suicide rate goes down!* He only said it once. But I just couldn't stop playing it over again in my head.

As we traveled around and did these shows, I could see what he meant. These soldiers and marines would pack the mess halls or makeshift auditoriums or bleachers outside on a soccer field just to hear us perform. They'd laugh and laugh and laugh and forget about their reality for ninety minutes.

The war was winding down then. It wasn't big news back home anymore. These soldiers were halfway across the world putting their lives on the line and feeling forgotten. They'd shake my hand or give me a hug. They'd thank me for coming and tell me it was the first time they'd laughed—really laughed—in a year. The next week, they might be rotating back to Iraq, to roadside bombs, to IEDs, to life and death balanced on a knife edge every day. In a place like that, I could really see what laughter meant to people. What I could do for them wasn't just a distraction; it was essential. It was life.

I remember doing a show at a dusty little outpost just a few miles from the Iraq border. To call it a *show* is actually an overstatement. There was no stage, no sound system, no organized seating. I am a big believer that the setting for comedy is hugely important, and these days, when I tour, I try to control as much of that as I can: I want the lighting done a certain way, the seating shouldn't be too far from the stage, and I bring audio and video with me. At this far-flung base, there was none of this, but somehow it was perfect. Me, standing on a wood pallet in the middle of the desert, telling jokes to a group of marines, roasting the other branches of the military, everyone howling with laughter. That's what comedy can do for people. Shoot, that's what it's done for me. There we were, in the desert during wartime, with unbearable heat, thick protective clothing, and uncomfortable seating. But for a few precious moments, we were somewhere else: We were in heaven, or at least as close as I've ever felt to it. That was comedy at its purest. Sometimes it can be that simple. And the feeling I got while perched on that pallet was the same exact feeling I got playing a sold-out arena. Arguably, even better.

The hard truth is, as much as I'd like to say that making those Marines laugh—or making a blind woman at a comedy club laugh or making a cancer patient in a hospital cackle at my videos—is what it's all about for me, it's not. It's part of it, a big part of it, but without that rush that comes with it, I wouldn't be trekking back and forth across the country, I wouldn't be flying to a forward-operating base in the desert, and I wouldn't be writing this book and trying to make the world see the real me. But I've come to understand that there's nothing wrong with that. It's okay to acknowledge, to own up to the less noble, less glamourous, more troubling sides of our humanity. In fact, it's vital. Trying to keep that stuff hidden is like carrying around a ticking time bomb in your back pocket: It's going to go off eventually, and when it does, your butt is going to get seriously torched. Trust me—I've got the scars to prove it.

About a year after I got back from Kuwait, I called the guy who had booked me on that tour and I asked if I could go back again. I told him how much the experience had meant to me, how just thinking about it had propelled me through some tough spells back at home. He was glad to hear that, but he explained that with most of the forces being withdrawn from Iraq, there weren't any plans for another tour to that region anytime soon.

"Don't worry, though," he told me. "We're waiting on another war. Fingers crossed."

Geez, I thought. I need comedy, but not *that* bad.

ABOUT THE AUTHOR

PHOTO: © Robby Klein

JOHN CRIST is a stand-up comedian from Lilburn, Georgia. Son of a preacher and one of eight homeschooled children, Crist had plenty of early inspiration to become a comedian. Most noted for his comedy videos that have garnered more than one billion views, Crist rose to popularity after several of his videos went viral, including "Every Parent at Disney," "If Football Coaches Were Honest," and "Lady Who Has a Bible Verse for Every Situation." His videos have been featured on the *Today Show, Fox & Friends,* and hundreds of other prominent outlets like *Sports Illustrated, USA Today,* and ESPN. Despite the success of these videos, Crist has never abandoned his original passion: live stand-up. His 2019 Human Being Tour ranked as Pollstar's fifteenth-largest comedy tour in the world. Crist lives in Nashville, Tennessee.